NICHIREN

[front

Kishio Satomi

Japanese Civilization

Its Significance and Realization; Nichirenism and Japanese National Principles

Simon Publications

2001

Library of Congress Control Number: 24008579

ISBN: 1-931313-93-8

Distributed by Ingram Book Company

Printed by Lightning Source Inc. La Vergne, TN

Published by Simon Publications, P.O. Box 321, Safety Harbor, FL 34695

INTRODUCTION

PROFESSOR SATOMI, although so far unknown in
England, is well known in Japan, both as an author of
works relating to Nichirenism and as the youngest son
of Mr. Chigaku Tanaka, the leading authority on the
life and writings of the apostle of Buddhist reformation. There is a powerful society in Japan, the
Kokuchukai, of which Mr. Chigaku Tanaka is the
president. It is composed entirely of laymen, and its
object is to present the ideal religious life, as revealed by
Nichiren, free from any obscurities which formalism
and the misdirected zeal of various sects may have
induced. The activities of this society are mainly
directed towards spreading the idea of practical religion
over every aspect of life, and bringing the religious
influence to bear not only on personal work like art
and science, but on the collective work of politics,
economics, and military affairs. Mr. Chigaku Tanaka
is the one who may be said to be the most active since
Nichiren's death in 1282 in spreading the doctrine, or
perhaps one ought rather to say the ideas, of Nichiren ;
and his son is an enthusiastic worker in the same field.

Of Nichiren's religion it may suffice to say here that
its main ideas are : the communion of those living
now and henceforth with all who have gone before,
and the restoration of primeval connection with the
eternal Buddha ; and that it is not the worship of an

abstract truth, but a life to be lived by every being, human or other, in the identity of man with nature. Nichiren was imbued with the strongest faith that Japanese Buddhism would spread from East to West, and his disciples are earnestly endeavouring to make his prophetic vision a present reality. The Nichirenians count their temples by thousands and their adherents by millions, and may claim recognition as one of the religious forces of the world.

G. F. BARWICK.

March, 1923.

AUTHOR'S PREFACE

THE harmonization of the civilization of the East with that of the West, is perhaps one of the most important tasks for the establishment of peace on any terms for which all the nations are longing. To accelerate this desired movement of ours, we must begin by sincerely and minutely studying these various civilizations. In the East, especially in Japan, Western civilization is extensively observed by the people, and fully adopted in recent times. While, according to my view, Eastern civilization, in spite of its being of great value, is studied in the West to a far less degree. It is a great pity. Eastern civilization developed mainly in the sphere of the spiritual aspect while Western civilization developed much more in material sciences.

The co-ordination of spiritualism and materialism is not only one of the problems in the history of philosophy, but it is a matter of fact of the world. For instance, still at the present day, the spirit of the Orient and that of the Occident are liable to clash in various ways, promoted largely by such influences as racial prejudice. But spiritualism and materialism are simply two aspects of one and the same thing. The unification, therefore, can be attained only by complete harmonization of the two. However, a thorough understanding of the Oriental civilization requires the most profound study for the following reasons:

Firstly, because it has not been much researched in Europe, and, secondly, because it is rooted in the deepest theory and it flourishes on the most solid and sincere practice. The spiritual civilization of the East must be studied by the European nations in addition to their own civilization. It is therefore our pleasant task to introduce our civilization to the West in gratitude for our indebtedness to their introduction of modern sciences.

The chief object of the present work is to make accessible to Western scholars and all people one of the very important aspects of Japanese spiritual civilization which is, in a sense, a result of our synthetic creation by harmonization and unification of several elements. The Author has treated Nichiren's Religion, known as the True Mahayana Buddhism, and the Japanese National Principles in this volume, to which he begs to draw the attention of readers.

There exist comparatively few works written by Western scholars introducing these problems, but we cannot expect perfect accuracy therein as far as present conditions are concerned. The present work is intended mainly for general readers, with a few exceptions which are intended for the convenience of scholars. Therefore, an excess of technical interpretations and discussions are omitted in this volume. I would point out that it is only a brief introduction to a most important problem, so that readers must not expect to find detailed information. It is to serve as prolegomena to another more lengthy and technical book of mine in English on these problems, to be published at a future date. Moreover, the present work was written under somewhat difficult conditions owing to my being abroad and being unable to secure suitable reference books.

Nevertheless, such having been the circumstances under which I wrote the present work, it will afford me the greatest pleasure if this small volume will take rank among the contributions of Western scholars and people. I began the draft of this book four months after my arrival in England from Japan and it has taken me just two months to bring it to completion. I am aware of the fact, therefore, that my English is far from being up to the standard of the language, which I sincerely trust readers will kindly tolerate. Many important problems dealing with the realization of the Japanese spiritual civilization are not dealt with in this present work, but these I hope to have a chance of introducing under a tentative title : "The Fundamental Ideas of Japanese Moral Philosophy."

My sincere acknowledgment is due to Mr. Chigaku Tanaka, my father in blood, the late president of the "Kokuchukai," whose results of researches gave rise to the revival of Modern Nichirenism, and I have freely adopted his theory in this book.

It is also my pleasant duty to appreciate the valuable suggestions and kindly help in English given to me by Mr. G. F. Barwick, the late Keeper of Printed Books of the British Museum.

K. SATOMI.

HARROW-ON-THE-HILL,
   ENGLAND.

CONTENTS

PRONUNCIATION OF JAPANESE WORDS

VOWELS :

    a has the sound of *a* in father.
    ai has the sound of *ai* in ails.
    i has the sound of *i* in ink.
    u has the sound of *u* in rule.
    e has the sound of *e* in prey.
    ei has the sound of *ei* in eight.
    o has the sound of *o* in so.
Long vowels are marked thus : ō, ū.

CONSONANTS :

    chi has the sound of *chi* in children.
    ts has the sound of *ts* in its.
    g is always hard.

Explanations of philosophical and other terms are given in the Glossarial Index (pp. 233–238).

JAPANESE CIVILIZATION
ITS SIGNIFICANCE AND REALIZATION

I

INTRODUCTORY

1. WHAT RELIGION IS

WHAT Religion is. What is Religion?

People were formerly and are still too egotistical in their conception of religion, and are liable to accept the fallacies that religion consists in going to church or in prayer, or that it is contained in the Bible or in other Scriptures as books, or even in preaching. But these ideas must be ascribed to ignorance, for even if people go to church and worship God, it is all in vain unless the prayer be pure and rational. I cannot conceive that there is a god so merciful and so accommodating as to listen to and unconditionally help people because of their various prayers, without considering the quality of the prayers themselves.

Man has the sentiment of dependence and of independence; the former is adaptation to some superhuman power and the latter is assimilation to his own self which means the extension of his personality. The former sentiment develops into a religious faith in a sense, but it is liable to fall into excess. For

B

instance, in this case, to pray to God with prayer which is devoid of rational judgment is indeed a comedy. Undoubtedly it comes from our own arbitrary interpretation.

It is very questionable whether religious faith as a mere psychical desire is always possible as the right faith. Of course, it is one of the tendencies of religious faith, nevertheless can we recognize it as a civilized religious faith, for a view which takes religion as a mere individual consolation is questionable. Let it be noted that serious consideration should be given thereto in order to understand religion. Many historical fallacies of religion are the outcome of such ideas.

So we must rid ourselves of any conception which looks upon religion as a function for the fulfilment of men's arbitrary will. Religious faith which is not supported by truth, or I should say irrational faith, always results in failure. It is useless to quibble about superstition still being a phenomenon of religious faith. But faith in a psychological sense does not always imply validity. A man in an electric car which has already derailed will exclaim with haughty air, " Didn't I get into the car ? " These two cases are parallel. The religion to be aimed at should be one of validity and value. If we were righteous there would be no necessity to ask God's help, for it is God's duty *a priori* to protect the righteous.

So, in the first place, " prayer " consists in " vowing " to do that which is righteous oneself and being benevolently inclined towards our fellow creatures and thereby engendering righteousness and perfect love.

In the second place, " prayer " also means " thanksgiving " for one's rectitude, and then again " prayer " should be a genuine feeling of absolute dependence on God. Otherwise contradiction will go on repeating itself everlastingly. The Great War, for instance, exposed to view the old Christian faith and the commonplace moral theory and showed them bankrupt in their very essence, because love and the *summum bonum* were invariably taught by religion and ethics in every connection, from olden times up to the present day. In spite of that, the so-called Sons of God fought the devil's battle with each other, for the Allied Nations and the Germans are the families and sons of the same God.

Jesus Christ says :

" Whosoever shall smite thee on thy right cheek, turn to him the other also " (Matthew and Luke).

The morality of such passive resistance is very questionable to me. But, then how came it about that the sons educated according to this non-resistance principle, acted against their merciful Father in contradiction to their own creed. Some of the sons prayed to God for victory, others for defeat. God, the common Father, must be embarrassed one would think when thus appealed to.

This would be a natural effect of Christianity in one direction. Individual Christians, Christian races and Christian societies are very much in evidence, nevertheless there exists no Christian State whatsoever. This originates in certain weak points of the Bible. Therefore the standard of salvation must be found in the religionizing of the State, not merely of individuals nor of the world in a vague sense.

Emancipate religion from old conceptions, from the Church and from the grave. The principle and spirit of religion should be interwoven with daily life. Strive to find religion at every step, at every turn, at work, at table, in business or in time of war or peace ! Plough the land for the sake of humanity, then shall a man find true happiness.

Human beings having been blinded by lust, viz. by the materialistic conceptions of history, which endeavoured to solve human existence merely with food and money, have degenerated. On the other hand, there were, and still are people who strive to realize an ideal human life by means of mere spiritualism. But such a one-sided opinion of life always leads the world into confusion and antagonism. Probably, we must acknowledge food and money or any other kind of material commodity in accordance with the realization of the Path (see Index). The signification of human life indeed exists in the vow of the practice of the Path, with the aid of material things.

This, of course, is the problem of our attitude and of our view of our life, and although some objections might be advanced, nevertheless, by such an attitude we ought to be able to produce harmonious human life, though it may appear to be a dogmatic view.

The so-called Truth is the Being as it is, accordingly it hardly becomes the standard of human life, while, the Path or the Way or the Morality is a reproduction of the Truth.

Obviously, therefore, it is the promise of mankind and the principle of the world, which is the product of long experience and of thought from all eternity. The promise or the principle judges men according to its own standard. There is no class or rank with reference to the authority of our existence.

Human beings can be classified into two kinds, viz. those who are Men of the Path and those who are not, consequently the protection and extension of the Path are the highest tasks of human life. The true religion of mankind must be the principle and power which will teach such conviction. Accordingly, religion must be understood as the principle and method of the synthetic creation connected with strong faith, which leads us even into fire and water if it is for the sake of the Path.

A religious faith which is merely a play of our sentiments, and not concerned with the task of the real reconstruction of life and of the world, will not be worthy of the future religion. Seeing that the principle or faith of religion and life is identical with the righteousness which does validate; this is how true religion is attained. Now let us add a few words and begin by asking ourselves, for instance, what is the object in worshipping God? Is it for oneself or is the purpose a charitable one? Naturally it should be the desire of mankind to prosper and be happy, but if religion should ever be devoted merely to the attainment of one's happiness and the promises of good fortune without having to strive for it, then it is devil's doctrine. Let us now consider the case of a thoughtless but enterprising person for whom faith is of no moment and who merely plays at religion traditionally. Suppose that, owing to carelessness, this individual meets with failure at every turn, and finding himself at the bottom of Fortune's wheel, feels the necessity of turning to

God in prayer. "In distress we turn to God," is then the expression. Can we acknowledge pure and righteous religious consciousness in such emotion, even though it be an inevitable weak point of human sentiment ? Is it not too selfish a point of view ?

A tradesman who is devoted to a religion and is a regular churchgoer in order to benefit by sermons and prayer, would appear to be a true believer of the religion as far as the church is concerned. He argues love, benevolence, truth, peace or something of the kind and over-estimates himself and is proud of his faith during those moments. However, when attending to his everyday duties he thinks of his own interests and competes with numerous other traders, gloats over his gains and should an opportunity offer, he would overthrow his competitors.

Is not such a view of peace a superficial one ? Can we recognize even the smallest degree of faith in such intentions ? Such a phenomenon is obviously contradictory. We cannot approve of such dualism or pluralism which draws a distinction between our mode of living and our religious faith.

Religion is neither a match-maker nor a funeral undertaker. The requiem and monkish nonsense may sound like golden words to one whose religion consists in empty formalism ; but do religious power and value exist in the verbosity of such professional religionists which is very often merely traditional and mercenary ?

The true value of religion is to be found only in quality, but neither in quantity nor in formalism. There are those who introduce the idea of rites, chanting, prayer and sermons whenever they think of religion. Now, however necessary these may be, they are merely formal attributes of religion. We must therefore seek the essential value of religion outside these. Now and again scholars are apt to convey the idea that religion consists in worship only, and not a few are imbued with this notion. They should reflect on the fact that their misconception originates in the meanings attached to the word " Religion."

Then what is the primary aim of a religion worthy of existence ? As a matter of course it is salvation, but is it intended to be in a spiritual sense only ? Salvation is pregnant with relief and redress of life and of the world, from the point of view of correlation of body and mind. Obviously therefore religion must take the whole life and world, spiritually and materially, as its objects in the process of salvation. Therefore religion must not be limited to the small sphere of interpretation. It is a fundamental fallacy that people in general hold the view of religion which is demonstrated above, and we need not be seriously concerned about those who think that their proper mission is fulfilled by the mere observance of forms and ceremonies. Religion must first of all take into consideration the whole personality, which is composed of three elements, i.e. reason, feeling and will. It is not sufficient that religion should relieve a man's feeling only, it must, at the same time, give rational and volitional satisfaction. According to this view, religion must imply the three elements synthetically ; so that it may be adaptable to any philosophy or science or new ideas, and it should be such as to give the right direction to be followed.

Moreover, religion should redeem the body as well. Because a man purified and idealized spiritually by religion, should gradually be idealized bodily in consequence. Human life is the process of attaining one's God, in other words, of proceeding from imperfect to perfect. It is indeed the application of Eugenics with the essential meaning of religion. According to my view, the Buddhist doctrine " Thirty-Two Signs (Lakchanas) " and " Eighty Excellent Specific Signs " has the signification of Eugenics. Thus, actual life is religion and religion is actual. The depravity of all religions from olden times to the present day has its root in the fallacy of a vague dualism of actual life and religion. Therefore religion is justified in leading and criticizing life in all its aspects. Religion must be woven into actual life, otherwise it would appear to be of no avail. In brief, the civilized religion worthy of the future must be the principle of the synthetic creation of life. Religion has the State and the world at large as well as the individual as objects of its salvation. But the unit of salvation is the State. In this respect religions in nine cases out of ten have vague ideas. The religion we need should assuredly be the authoritative principle of our actual life, and of course that of the countries and the world as well.

In this connection I am going to introduce Nichiren's religion as the representative one of Japan. I have stated thus a part of my ideas about religion from a common sense point of view. My scientific and philosophical studies of religion in general will be published on some future occasion.

2.   RECONSTRUCTION OF THE WORLD

The present world, without doubt, has come to a deadlock.   There exist religion, ethics, philosophy, art, science, politics, law, the church, schools, sages, priests, teachers and scholars ; but how powerless these are ! The teachings of the sages have pervaded the world, nevertheless the human race has degenerated after being perplexed by this one or that one. People have sought liberty, equality and philanthropy and they are still seeking ; nay, instead of liberty restriction has been their lot, and while searching for equality they have found inequality after all ; and they are still self-contradictory in their garment of philanthropy.   The Buddha Shakamuni, Jesus Christ, Socrates, Confucius and the other sages or men of wisdom, all aimed at leading man to supreme goodness and absolute peace.

Their adherents in the world might be types of righteousness, even though the world at large has degenerated ceaselessly ; but verily the teachings of these sages have resulted in complete failure. We are aware that there exist many true Christians, true Buddhists and other men of lofty character, but how are we to deal with this impure world at large ? And again there are also many books in which the highest standard of goodness is taught ; but devolution is apparent even here, in this dissolute world. However hard people may struggle for idealism, if they do not consider this point, then all their efforts will prove abortive.

Alas, the so-called civilization exhibits its skilfulness

in killing man, and some of its outstanding inventions are warships, guns, poison-gas, tanks and so forth. The Great War, as already mentioned, is the gratification of human greediness, bellicosity and querulous folly which have accumulated in the course of several thousand years. The League of Nations or the International Peace Conference is, it is true, an outcome of the Great War. Of course there were people who had been looking for peace, but it was not a universal yearning. Now at last the time is ripe for the reformation of the world.

Many problems of the world of to-day, such as the reduction of armaments or international peace conferences and schemes of like nature, are preliminary steps towards the creating of the new world, but, primarily, this new world must be built on a solid foundation. People may have infinite longing for perfect peace, yet every effort will prove futile unless all endeavours are in earnest for the sake of the true value of life. The present tendency of the nations, at any rate, is worthy of being called progress. We must bring about in the near future an international constitution so that the States and the world may be judged. It is illogical that a State should punish an individual man or woman for a theft or other crime of which the State itself is guilty on a much larger scale. It is out of all reason to ascribe equity to national greediness. Therefore the State must undergo a moral reconstruction. So we must contrive to bring about a reconstruction of the world, its countries and its individuals. We offer Nichirenism and the Japanese National Principles as the means to be considered by the nations.

3. WHAT NICHIRENISM IS

Nichirenism, which I am going to sketch briefly in this work, originates from the name of a great Japanese Buddhist, viz. Nichiren, who lived about seven hundred years ago. He is, indeed, the man of the revolution of Buddhism, and I may say of all religions in a sense. His thought, his doctrine and its practice, faith, prophecy and miracles, if any, are clearly illustrated in the four hundred articles of his works. Above a quarter of the works extant are found in his own handwriting, so that all researches can be made by scholars palæographically about him and his surroundings.

It deserves to be called a miracle that a great religionist's manuscripts have remained in good preservation for more than seven hundred mortal years. With reference to this, we cannot compare Nichiren with other religionists whose teachings have been handed down from the ancient peoples, and, moreover, have been modified by their followers in ninety-nine cases out of one hundred.

Nichirenism is the principle of the synthetic creation based on Nichiren's doctrine, thought and faith, and it is religion in quite an ordinary sense, but at the same time it is the general basis of life and of the world. Accordingly, we cannot treat Nichirenism as a mere form of Buddhism, however apt we may be to allow our views to be influenced by our prejudices and our sectarianism when we come in touch with a sect which is foreign to us. So, to begin with, when seeking truth, we must eliminate sectarianism, which of itself alone will confuse our understanding or reason. For this cause and also in order to free Nichiren's religion from the hackneyed conception of religion, we use the appellation Nichirenism, the term adopted by Chigaku Tanaka.

Nichirenism, in the first place, rejects all other religions on the one hand, but, on the other hand, approves them all, when enlightened and elucidated by Nichirenism. From the former point of view, Nichirenism is not incompatible with the other religions, but is in unison and harmony with them from the latter point of view.

Nichirenism was founded seven hundred years ago, but it could not fully develop in the unfavourable political circumstances of the time. Japan, in other words, was not given suitable conditions for the acceptance of Nichirenism, because she was ruled by despotic governments. Nichirenians of all ages have endeavoured to reform the country to her ideals and have counselled the government and the people.

All the governments, with hardly an exception, severely harassed it. Extension was out of the question ; Nichirenism narrowly escaped ruin and was obliged to apostatize from its true spirit to an entirely different one. About half a century ago the late Great Emperor Meiji established the Japanese Constitution, and religious tolerance became a matter of fact. Hereupon, Japan prepared to accept Nichirenism freely.

The revival of pure Nichirenism, properly founded on Nichiren's works, took place within the last forty years or thereabouts, after the appearance of Chigaku Tanaka, and the spread of Nichirenism in the present day is due to Tanaka's continuous activity. Be that as it may, the time is now opportune for the propagation of Nichirenism throughout the world.

Nichirenism is by no means the religion of the past, but the religion of the future and for ever. The past ages were not ready to be Nichirenized for many reasons, the political condition was one of them, the state of civilization was another, and the affairs of the world of thought might also be added. But now the world has come to a standstill, so that it must of necessity take a new turn.

II

FIVE CRITICAL PRINCIPLES

1. Buddhist Criticism

ALL Buddhist Sects, except the Zen Sect, have their own criticism or critical doctrine, which is their doctrinal demonstration for the establishment of their sects, in spite of the existence of earlier sects.

The critical doctrine as a matter of course came into existence after the establishment of many schools and theories. *Chiko* (Sanskrit. Iñanaprabha) in India, was the first systematizer of critical doctrine, and at his suggestion *Ekwan* was the first to initiate it in China, and then *Shūai, Kyu-Hosshi, Kajo, Hōun* and *Ji-on*, etc., followed suite, and finally the great Master *Tendai*, who established the critical doctrine, successfully dividing it into what is called " Five Epochs and Eight Doctrines."

All kinds of critical doctrines tried to establish the authoritative principle of Buddhism according to certain methods, and to show cause for establishing a new sect (Satomi, "New Study of Nichirenism," pp. 248–259. In Japanese).

The criticism of Nichirenism is what is called " Five Critical Principles." Nichiren attained an enlightenment after a long research spread over twenty years, and systematized the Five Critical Principles as the result of his four careful perusals of all the Buddhist Scriptures. He agreed with Tendai's critical doctrine, " Five Epochs and Eight Doctrines " to a certain extent, but he deepened and widened the method from his *unique point of view* (which is the subject of this work), and established the perfect criticism on the authority of his conviction of *Honge Jogyo* by his religious practice of the *Hokekyo*.

His criticism, when observing both the general effect and the minute details of Buddhism, has five aspects, explained as follows, according to the suggestion by Chiō Yamakawa of the *Kokuchukai :*

(1) Comparative study of Buddhist doctrines.
(2) Psychological research into the people's capacity for Buddhism.
(3) Sociological study of the times.
(4) State-ethnical study of religious influence.
(5) Evolutionistic study of Buddhism.

He was actuated by the following phrase of the Hokekyo, and he established this critical doctrine at Izu when he was exiled there by the Hojos government. It says :

" He will, after Buddha's Death, unravel (or know) the origin and orders, and he will preach the law as it is according to the real signification of the Buddhist Scriptures " (Yamakawa's Japanese translation, p. 567 ; cf. Kern, p. 369).

Nichiren writes in his article, " Analogue of Wise and Foolish," " First of all, doctrine, capacity, the times, the country and retrocession and progress (or

Backward and Forward) of religious distribution must be evident in order to propagate Buddhism and to benefit mankind " (*Shōgu Mondō-shō*, Works, p. 223 ; cf. pp. 262–263, p. 1383).

How wonderful it is that so thorough a system for the study of religion has been established by him seven hundred years ago. Now let us go through the Five Critical Principles.

2. DOCTRINE

He formulated at the outset, *Five degrees of comparison*, viz. (1) Buddhism and Brahmanism, etc. (2) Mahayana Buddhism and Hinayana Buddhism. (3) Hokekyo and all other Buddhist Scriptures. (4) The former fourteen chapters of the Hokekyo and the latter fourteen chapters. (5) Formal Doctrine and Introspection or Intuition. He learned the entire Indian philosophy and religion, also Confucianism and other Chinese philosophy in his youth. He compared all such topics with Buddhism in general, and came to the conclusion that all these have evolved into Buddhism.

He then compared Mahayana Buddhism with Hinayana Buddhism. If we look at it in the domain of Buddhist Scriptures it is the comparison of the Agāma Scriptures and all the Mahayana Scriptures ; and in the sphere of sects, it is the comparison of the three sects (*Kusha, Jōjits, Rits*) and those of *Sanron, Hosso, Kegon, Shingon, Tendai* and others (Suzuki: " Outlines of Mahayana Buddhism." McGovern: " An Introduction to Mahayana Buddhism, etc.").

N.B.—There are two popular and authoritative

editions of Nichiren's works at present. The one is *Ryōgonkaku* edition, by Kato and assistants, the other, the *Shishiō Bunko* edition, compiled and annotated by Nagataki and Yamakawa, under the superintendence of Chigaku Tanaka. The former takes the chronological system and the latter the subject system of arrangement ; both editions are founded on Taido Ogawa's compilation. In the present work the author quotes from the *Shishiō Bunko* edition with a few exceptions.

As a matter of fact Nichiren preferred the Mahayana Buddhism *par excellence*. After making his selection he went on further comparing the teachings of pious imposition and the true teachings or, more properly, general and specific Mahayana Buddhism. He had come to know that the Hokekyo alone is the true teaching of Buddha and that all the rest are simply for the purpose of pious imposition (the end sanctifies the means), so he adopted the Hokekyo as the authority. For in all the Scriptures, except the Hokekyo, there is no principle enabling man to become God, because they do not evince the Mutual Participation of the Ten Worlds. Moreover, they look upon Buddha Shakamuni merely as having been born in India and become Buddha six years after he left the castle of Gaya. In other words, these are their two fundamental weak points. Thus Nichiren made the Hokekyo his basis, without however neglecting the examination of the Hokekyo itself. He made the comparison between the two parts of the Hokekyo ; the *Shakumon*, which is composed of the first fourteen chapters, and the *Honmon*, the remaining fourteen chapters of the Scripture. The one defective point

c

which disregarded the Mutual Participation is eliminated in the Shakumon of this Scripture, but there remained one more weak point which I have already mentioned. Therefore he gave up the Shakumon in favour of the Honmon. Thus he championed the cause of the Honmon, and lastly he compared Introspection and Practice with Doctrine, and of course he acknowledged the superiority of the Introspection and Practice of the Hokekyo.

Then, again, he established another method for the classification of Buddhism, namely "The Fivefold Three Divisions." At first he applied this method to the whole of Buddhism, which produced the Introductory Portion to which Hihayana Buddhism and all the general Mahayana Buddhism belong, the Main Portion to which the Hokekyo belongs, and the Subordinate Portion to which the Nehangyo belongs.

Secondly, the division has reference to the Hokekyos, which are in three parts, viz. the *Muryogikyo* the prolegomena, the Hokekyo the main portion and the *Kan-Fugenkyo* the subordinate portion. (See Pt. II, Chap. VII.)

According to this method, he divided the Shakumon and the Honmon of the Hokekyo into three parts in accordance with the real signification, and eventually he determined on the Sacred Title of the Hokekyo as the ultimate teaching of them all. He divided also the Sacred Title, which is the essential principle of the Hokekyo, into three aspects. All the Buddhist Scriptures, even the Hokekyo, are the Introductory Portion, the Sacred Title is the Main Portion of all Buddhism. But as for the subordinate portion thereof, he did not determine so definitely as in the above examples. So this problem was one of serious question throughout seven hundred consecutive years, but some twenty years ago Chigaku Tanaka demonstrated this problem in one of his works ("*Honge Shōshaku Ron*," i.e. "Two methods of Buddhist Propagation," pp. 133–156). According to him, the subordinate portion of the Sacred Title, the essential principle, is Nichiren's religious practice itself. Nobody has disputed this solution since his theory appeared. Of course, it must be suggested by Nichiren himself ; I will quote one of Nichiren's suggestions on this problem which was first cited by Tanaka.

"The Introductory portion, the main portion and the subordinate portion of the Honmon are all mentioned at the beginning of the Latter Days " (Nichiren, Works, p. 98).

Thus Nichiren arranged the whole of Buddhism in systematic order from the doctrinal point of view, and he confirmed all about the position and the value of the Hokekyo throughout Buddhism.

I feel that it behoves me to say a few more words concerning the doctrine Nichiren adopted as aforesaid (p. 16), namely the Great Master Tendai's criticism, which is named "Five Epochs and Eight Aspects of Doctrines." According to Tendai, there are eight aspects possible concerning Buddha's Law. Namely, four classes of doctrine proper and four modes of instruction. In addition, Tendai founded another solid method of research which he called "Three Forms of Doctrine." Nichiren adopted all these systems of Tendai to a certain extent under his own authority. Tendai's theory is the foundation of Nichirenism, properly speaking, as will appear more fully later on.

3. CAPABILITY

After the examination of doctrine, Nichiren had, as his next object, the ascertainment of man's capability for the observance of religion. He investigated all kinds of religious capabilities from ancient times until his own day, and he took account of relations between religion and capabilities being in harmony. In other words, he thought that religion would be futile, despite all efforts, unless in sympathy with man's capabilities. He classified every kind of capability into the eight following categories :

<table>
<tr><td rowspan="8">Capabilities</td><td>1. Prompt perception.</td></tr>
<tr><td>2. Gradual perception.</td></tr>
<tr><td>3. Secret perception.</td></tr>
<tr><td>4. Indefinite perception.</td></tr>
<tr><td>5. Casual perception.</td></tr>
<tr><td>6. Common perception.</td></tr>
<tr><td>7. Independent or isolated perception.</td></tr>
<tr><td>8. Perfect perception.</td></tr>
</table>

From 1 to 4 concern religious motives, and from 5 to 8 the nature of religious capabilities. This table shows his analysis of religious capability in general. We will, however, describe the capability and tendency in the days of the Latter Law, leaving out the commentary on the above table. With reference to the Latter Law Nichiren studied both sides simultaneously, individuals and the times and society. Readers, therefore, must carefully read the next section wherein we comment on the times.

To begin with, he saw the evil side and classified it as follows :

Ten Evils	1 Destruction of living beings	body
	2 Stealing	
	3 Adultery	
	4 lying	mouth
	5 ornamentation	
	6 vilification	
	7 insincerity or duplicity	
	8 greediness	heart
	9 jealousy accompanied with fury	
	10 folly—querulousness	

Five treacheries	1 parricide	destruction of morality
	2 matricide	
	3 murdering of men of wisdom and sages (Arhan)	
	4 disturbing the harmony of religionists	destruction of religion
	5 shedding Buddha's blood	

Fourteen disparagements of the truth	1 arrogance	psychic
	2 idle negligence	
	3 self-righteousness	
	4 superficial recognition	
	5 persistence in avarice	
	6 incomprehension	thoughtful
	7 unbelief	
	8 frowning	
	9 suspicion	
	10 abuse	
	11 slighting goodness	moral
	12 hating goodness	
	13 jealousy of goodness	
	14 grudging goodness	

These Evils have gone on existing from ancient times, but have been ever increasing in the days of the Latter Law. The fourteen disparagements of the truth are the worst evils, and do not merely destroy relative morality, but at the same time the very truth itself. He, therefore, thought that the latter ones are the worst among the three kinds.

" How much more is it the case after Buddha's Death." This phrase foretells such an increase of evils in the Latter Days.

The five Treacheries are not merely a simple exposure of evil nature and destruction of morality, like the Ten Evils, but rather mean persecution for those who observe the truth. The Fourteen disparagements of the truth, too, are not mere evils as has been already mentioned. These two are beyond the power of common religions; therefore they are excepted even among the Forty-Eight Invocations of Amida Buddha (see the *Muryogikyo*; Aparimitāyus-Sūtra; and Works, p. 318).

The capability of people in the days of the Latter Law applies to the Hokekyo only, which he decided according to the proof of the Scriptures. Still, he divided the capability of the Hokekyo into two types; the one is meek capability and the other treacherous, and both are included in the account. The treacherous capability is mentioned in Chapter XIII of the Hokekyo, viz. self-conceited people of a lower order, self-conceited religionists and scholars, and self-conceited priests under the mask of sages.

On the one hand, Nichiren accepted " Four instructive methods " (Japanese, *Shi-shits-dan*, Skt. Siddhānta), which were adopted in the general Buddhism, but, on the other hand, he chose mainly the " Three Benefits," comprising " Seed-Benefit, Maturity-Benefit and Harvest-Benefit." In particular, he defended the cause of Seed-Benefit, which means to put Buddha-Seed into the field of mind.

In the Buddhist Doctrine the idea of Buddha-Seed

is divided into two parts, the one is named " Seed in respect of one's nature " and the other " Seed in regard to instructive guidance." Of course, even people of the Latter Days have Divine-Nature or Buddha-Nature fundamentally in their character, in other words, unconscious Buddha-Seed still exists ; also conscious Buddha-Seed which is rendered active by teaching and by their religious practice (" Opening the Eyes," Works, p. 57).

The so-called Seed-Benefit means causing strong vibrations in people's unconscious Buddha-Seed and lifting it and setting it in motion. For there exists in everybody the utmost delusive ignorance (or nescience, Skt. avidyā māyā), therefore it must be vigorously awakened (Works, pp. 336, 258–259).

We must even go a step further on this point, comparing the conditions of society at that period.

4. THE TIMES

We cannot decide what religion is suitable for the people from a mere individual psychological view. What has to be taken into consideration is the tendency of the times or society. Nichiren, therefore, proceeds with his researches according to the times, the background of the people (Works, pp. 107–120).

Nichiren, hereupon, examined throughout all the Scriptures corresponding with the times, and thus he found how to propagate and extend the Hokekyo-centric religion.

According to him, the world, at that time, un-fortunately realized the prophecy of Five Turbidities, written about in the second chapter of the Hokekyo. What are the Five Turbidities ? They are :

   1. Turbidity or Impurity of thought.
   2.   ,,   of lust or instinct.
   3.   ,,   of the times.
   4.   ,,   of body and soul.
   5.   ,,   of life.

The former three conditions are the cause of the latter two, and it seemed to him that in such evil times the sole authoritative religion which can adequately reconstruct such a world is the Hokekyo-centric religion. But it will be clearer to readers if they are given an idea of the Hokekyo before knowing about the times in detail. Let us, therefore, defer this problem until we come to Chapters XII and XIII in this book.

5. COUNTRY

What is the country or the state ? I venture to say that the state is the fundamental civilization. Well, civilization of a human kind can be classified in two categories.

Philosophy, religion, science, art and all others belong to the effectual civilization, while the state is the cause. This has been clearly demonstrated in the history of civilization. No effective instrument of civilization could appear without the protection of the country. The Roman civilization, the Greek civilization, the Indian, and the Chinese or the like, one and all of them flourished in the palmy days of the respective countries. When states have been overthrown and ruined their civilizations have ceased concomitantly. Did not the Greek and then the Roman civilizations fare in that manner ? Did not the glorious Indian civilization almost go to ruin ? Did not also the Chinese civilization perish ? Can we still find the flower and essence of Buddhism in India to-day, albeit that it first came to light in India ? Or again, can we find in China to-day true Confucianism and Buddhism both of which originated or were fully developed in China ? Unfortunately these civilizations left their lands of birth from the day of their fall, but they have been completely regenerated overseas in Japan. In this sense the state is the cradle and home of individual civilization.

Nichiren, therefore, took the country as the next subject for his critical research. He thought that all the conditions of the state were connected with religion ; for instance, climate, race, production, position, domain, religions, morality and history and so forth. Taking all these conditions into consideration he looked to Japan as the proper country where the Hokekyo-centric religion could be developed and authorized. At the same time he was much interested in the fact of the " Gradual transmission of Buddhism to the East," a fact that many sages had prophesied ; as, for instance, Miroku (Maitreya) said :

" There is a small country in the East Sea where alone capability for Mahayana Buddhism exists," and *Choko* said to the effect that :

" This canon is fraught with the destiny of a small country in a north-eastern direction."

He cited these two phrases, and a few others in one of his letters to Lord Nanjō (Works, p. 279).

Hence Nichiren determined on Japan, and found her to be the very land for the establishment of the ideal of the Hokekyo.

The essence of Buddhism, after once having been collected and completed in Japan, is to go out on its final mission to the whole world. Hence he says in his " On my realization of Buddha's Prophecy " :

" The Moon rises in the west and shines on the east, the Sun rises in the east and shines on the west. Buddhism, too, is just like this (or observed like this ; the original is ' *Denji*,' which means to impart and practice). It developed from west to east during two thousand years of the Right and Fanciful Laws, but, in the Latter Days, it is to go from east to west. The Great Master *Myōraku* says: Are they in truth not seeking True Buddhism on one of four directions, knowing that they have lost Buddhism in India ? This means that there is no Buddhism in India.

" In China, over 150 years have passed since *Hokuteki* captured *Tonkin* (Tungking) in the dynasty of *Kōsō*, and Buddhism and the state have come to an end there, at any rate. In China, the Hinayana Scriptures do not exist at all, and the Mahayana Scriptures were all but lost, so *Jakusho* and others transferred those Scriptures to China from Japan. But there was no man who accepted and *observed* the Scriptures ; but many were like stones or pieces of wood, lifeless, though wearing clothing. Hence, says *Junshiki :* At the beginning Buddhism was transformed from West to East, similarly to the moon rising in the West and setting in the East. Just as these words are true, it is likewise true that Buddhism has ceased to exist in China " (Works, pp. 475–6).

Nichiren firmly believed that the doctrine of the Hokekyo and Japanese National Principles, in other words, both the nature of Japan and that of the Hokekyo have innate relation *a priori*.

The Hokekyo must have a state like Japan in order to validate its pregnant value, and Japan should have the Hokekyo for the sake of the realization of her national ideal. Therefore, Nichiren praised Japan in regard of the truth of the Hokekyo from the doctrinal point of view, not for the sake of his fatherland. We must thoroughly examine this problem and it will be discussed in subsequent chapters.

6. ORDERS

Before a new religion is created, all historical religions must be taken into serious consideration ; therefore Nichiren finally directed his attention to all religions of the past upon which he had good reason to establish his own religion. Buddhism, for example, underwent a course of evolutional development. First of all, Hinayana Buddhism spread, followed by General Mahayanism and lastly Specific Mahayanism of the Hokekyo came into existence. Now just let us give the following illustration :—

Primitive human beings had lower nature-religions, viz. nature worship, totemism, animal worship, phallicism and litholatry, etc. ; and this period was succeeded by higher nature-religions such as the Vedic religion, the Ancient Greek religion and the

Ancient Persian religion ; these, again, were replaced by quasi-ethical religions, and such. Nature religions were then abandoned for more purely ethical religions. So we must not lose sight of the historical development of religion. Nichiren has to a considerable extent devoted himself to the comparative study of rites, reference books and schools, and to Hinayana as well as Mahayana Buddhism. Thus he found that the time was propitious for accepting the Hokekyo-centric religion when Buddhism had attained full development.

Of course we cannot permanently adhere to Hinayana Buddhism, but naturally desire to go a step farther towards Mahayana Buddhism ; nor can we remain satisfied with general Mahayanism, but aspire to the highest form of Buddhism. It is obviously a great anachronism to propagate primitive religion in the civilized world. Surely times and religions ought to be concurrent. Religions which are in accordance with the times must reflect on past ages on the one hand, but, nevertheless, must be keenly observant of the future. Hence his evolutionistic theory. On the strength of the above elucidation let us quote one of Nichiren's own writings thereupon :

" I venture to say that he who would propagate true Buddhism after having discerned these Five Principles is worthy to be called the national leader of Japan. Therefore, one who knows the Hokekyo to be the King of all the Buddhist Scriptures, is the man capable of knowing true Buddhism. . . .

" Thousands of scholars go astray in this relation. There are few men who know true Buddhism."

Not to know the true religion would mean not to have

read the Hokekyo. If no one had read the Hokekyo, there could be no master of the state. Without a master of the nation people would hardly be able to discriminate between Mahayana and Hinayana Buddhism, Scriptures of means and purpose, exoteric and esoteric Buddhism, and they would get no relief. Eventually they would become traitors to the truth. Thereby there would be a great many more people who would descend into the Nethermost Hell by means of Buddhism than there are grains of sand and dust. Or to express it differently, fewer men than particles of dust on finger-nails would be released by observing Buddhism (*Kyō-ki-ji-koku-shō*, " Essay on Doctrines, Capability, Times and Country," Works, p. 264).

7. ON THE HOKEKYO

If ever Japan produced a religious man worthy of the name, Nichiren was the man. He felt convinced that he was the incarnation of *Honge Jogyo* (Skt. Viśiṣṭa-Cāritra) throughout the experiences and practices of his religious life. Now the so-called Honge Jogyo is the man who was foretold by Buddha Shakamuni (Skt. Śakyamuni) in the Hokekyo or *Myō-hō-renge-kyō* (Skt. Saddharmapundarka-sūtra), and it is my duty to offer my tribute of respect to the Hokekyo itself.

It is, of course, an established fact that the Hokekyo is the highest development of Buddhism. If the Hokekyo is not contained in Buddhism, then, even though there exist therein seven thousand Scriptures, all these books are but contradictory teachings. therefore when a man desires to make a study of

Buddhism, it is absolutely necessary for him to learn the position of the Hokekyo in all Buddhist Scriptures. There are many translations of this Scripture in the world, both in the East and in the West. But the translation "*par excellence*" we consider from doctrinal and exegetic standpoints to be "The *Myō-hō-renge-kyō*" text, translated by Kumarajū (or Kumaragiva) in 407. In Japan there are three Chinese translations extant ; the title of the first is "The *Sho-Hokekyo*," of the second "The *Myohorengekyo*" and of the third "The *Tenbon Myohorengekyo*." The *Sho-Hokekyo* and the *Tenbon Myohorengekyo* agree with the extant Sanscrit texts in their main systems and characters. With reference to this, Kern's English and Burnouf's French translations agree also. Now, I can imagine that there are some who will prefer the Sanscrit text because it is an original one, and for them the above-mentioned translations, with the exception of Kumaraju's, might be accepted as the most trustworthy authorities of our times.

But on the whole, according to Yamakawa, we can arrange all the sacred books in two types, namely the systematic Scriptures and the fragmentary ones. For instance the Bible or the Analecta of Confucius belongs to the fragmentary sacred books, but the Buddhist Scriptures, as a rule, belong to the systematic ones. The fragmentary Scriptures are in nine cases out of ten full of those words or phrases which at once produce ennobling incitements to the reader's moral feelings. On the contrary, while the systematic Scriptures contain such moments in a smaller degree they reveal to the reader the systematic understanding of the world or life. Of course, this classification has nothing to do with the estimation in which they are held, for the fragmentary Scriptures are not always less valuable than others and vice versa. But whenever we read sacred books we must first of all have this idea of their main characteristics in our minds.

The Hokekyo cannot be understood without paying due attention to its wonderful system. Indeed, above all, the Hokekyo contains a gigantic world theory in the very system itself. If we consider the letter of the Scripture only, we may perhaps find it impossible to understand what it really is; consequently in determining the best text of the Scripture, a thorough investigation of the system must be made. From this point of view I consider that Kumaraju's translation is the best that has yet appeared.

As regards the texts of the Hokekyo, I cannot go into details in this book, but, by the way, let us briefly discuss one of the problems. Now all the translations, except the Myohorengekyo, have determined the chapter of Entrusting (*Zokurui-Hon*) as being the last chapter (Kern's English translation, p. 446, Vol. XXI, the S.B.E., Oxford University). On the other hand, in the Myohorengekyo, " the Entrusting " is classified as the twenty-second, and is followed by six more chapters.

According to Dr. Kern's view these six chapters are simply later additions; but I am sorry to say I am not of his opinion, for we believe firmly that all extant Sanscrit texts which determine " the Entrusting " as the last chapter are nothing more nor less than the disordered ones. We must, however, defer any further discussion of this matter to another opportunity.

First of all, we must investigate the system. If the chapter of " Entrusting " is the last one, it becomes impossible to perceive the consistent development of the construction, and the dramatic performance of the Scripture. There are two evident divisions in the Scripture, viz. the first fourteen chapters from I to XIV, which are called " *Shaku-Mon*," and the remaining fourteen chapters which are called " *Hon-Mon*." Let us contrast the characteristics of these two parts.

The idea of the former is a sort of mechanism and of the latter teleologism; and again, the one is philosophical, realistic, inductive, comparative and materialistic, while the other is religious, idealistic, deductive, dogmatic and spiritualistic. Then those two opposite tendencies are blended into a consistent harmony in a systematic course. Two renowned scholars, Tendai, the Great Master in China, and Dengyo, the Great Master in Japan, are the chief authorities in the School of the Hokekyo, and at the same time they are known as the forerunners of Nichiren. But there is a great difference in their attitudes towards the Hokekyo. Nichiren based his position on the latter, the Honmon, but Tendai and Dengyo adopted the former, the Shakumon; theory being accepted by them, whereas Nichiren accepted practice seriously; the difference being due to their different missions and times. Such differences between two parts of the Scriptures do actually exist; and there are still other classifications from the taxonomical point of view, for instance, the Japanese term " *San -ne* " means Three Meetings, as follows :

From the beginning to X is termed " *Zen-Ryozen-e*,"

from X to XXII "*Koku-e*" and the remaining six chapters "*Go-Ryozen-e.*" *Zen-Ryozen-e* means the early sermons on the peak of Gijihakuta (Pali) or Gṛdhrakuta (Sanscrit), now called Chata; *Koku-e,* the middle preachings in Heaven; and Go-Ryozen-e, the later sermons on Gṛdhrakuta again; the most important parts were developed during the middle preachings in heaven.

Therefore you will find, if you read the Hokekyo carefully, that there are many complicated changes in these three preachings. And again, we can classify the system from another point of view; the introductory portion, the main portion and the subordinate portion. Furthermore it is necessary for the classification to be carried one step further in order to apply these three gradual divisions to the whole system, i.e. to the Shakumon and to the Honmon. But it would be difficult and troublesome for the reader to grasp, so we will add a note on the three gradual divisions of the Honmon only.

According to this method of division, Chapter XV forms the introduction; from the latter half of Chapter XV to the first half of Chapter XVIII is the body; and the remainder is the concluding portion. But it is to be noted that "the concluding portion of the Honmon returns again to the Shakumon with reference to the internal significance."

Anyone who will appreciate these statements and look into the system will understand what a wonderful system it is!

Even though a scholar may be proud of his knowledge of the Hokekyo, unless he takes account of the system, I venture to say that his reading is practically

D

in vain. There is no doubt that Buddha himself repudiated all the sermons which he preached prior to the Hokekyo. We must take into account that there exists one scripture which was preached as the prolegomena or introductory scripture to the Hokekyo, entitled " *Muryogikyo* " (Skt. Amitārtha-sūtra). In the second chapter thereof, Buddha says :

" I did not reveal the truth during these forty years."

The *Muryogikyo* shows that all the preachings of Buddha prior to the Hokekyo are intended to help the understanding of the true Buddhism, which could not be preached in early days owing to the rudimentary culture of the people. Therefore Buddha preached many different theories for the sake of training, and he tried all means in order to make people capable of accepting His true teaching. Moreover, it is mentioned in the same chapter thereof that those innumerable significations which were sermonized prior to the Hokekyo, emanated from the One Truth, and the One Truth is nothing but " Suchness."

But he did not sermonize about the " Suchness " in detail in that scripture, for he sinks into deep meditation as soon as the above preaching ends. He is going to reveal the truth as to how the pulpits of the Hokekyo open.

In the chapter " Introduction " in the Hokekyo, the significant purport of the preaching of the Scripture is stated in idealized words. He afterwards elucidated the true value of *human nature as it is* for the first time in the second chapter. It is the unique theory

and is different from all other Scriptures. The few
essential lines of it are :

" The Law which Buddha attained to perfection
is most rare and difficult to understand. None but
between a Buddha and a Buddha truth of reality is
unravelled. It is what I call Such Forms, Such
Natures, Such Bodies, Such Powers, Such Functions,
Such Dynamic Causes, Such Statistic Causes, Such
Effects, Such Retributions and Such Consummate
and Consistent Unities of Origin and End of all
Beings " (Yamakawa, p. 42 ; see Kern, p. 32).

According to Tendai this doctrine is termed
" Mutual Participation of the Ten Worlds," that is to
say, Buddha classified human nature into ten worlds
from Buddha to Hell. The possibility of the approxi-
mation of every being to the mortal Buddha was not
admitted in any previous Scriptures, while in the
Hokekyo it became clear that every being has the
nature of Buddha or the divine essence in his very
soul. So, if he looks within himself for his hidden
treasure, namely the intrinsic value of personality,
and leads it to realization, then he can make himself
Buddha. Because these ten worlds participate in one
another ten times ten. Hence the theory of " Mutual
Participation." If so, why such different worlds ?
Tendai and Nichiren explained it by " Tenfold Suchness," Japanese technic " Jūnyo," i.e. ten categories
like the following :

    1. Form or Essence (*So*).
    2. Nature or Attribute (*Sho*).
    3. Body or Manifestation (*Tai*).

4. Energy or Power or Potency (*Riki*).
5. Movement or Function (*Sa*).
6. Dynamic Cause (*In*).
7. Statistic Cause (*En*).
8. Effect (*Kwa*).
9. Retribution or Compensation (*Ho*).
10. Consummate and Consistent Unity of Origin and End (*Hon-mats Kukyō Tow*).

This causality or mutuality, "Tenfold Suchness of Reality," shows the differences as such ten worlds. Each of the ten are interrelated to each, and make a hundredfold worlds, and if each of these has the inter-relation with "Tenfold Suchness," then "A Thousand-fold Suchness"; and again if it is correlated with "Three States of the Body and Spirit," we then have "Three Thousandfold worlds." The Three States of the body and spirit (Japanese, *San Seken*, i.e. three kinds of the world) are nothing but another view of the world in Buddhism. This is shown in the following table :

I. All living creatures.
II. Earth or Land.
III. Five accumulated essences of the human body.

1. Substance.
2. Perception.
3. Conception.
4. Action.
5. Knowledge.

It is wonderful that all these worlds are inherent in our minds; and this doctrine is termed "*Ichinen*

Sanzen," meaning " Three thousand Worlds inherent in one person."

The theory which I have shown above was developed in the former fourteen chapters, the Shakumon. But the problem of Buddha Shakamuni's personality is still unsolved. In Chapter XVI (Kern, XV, p. 298), Buddha revealed and enlightened His personality with vigorous tone as Eternal Tathagata.

In the third chapter, Buddha preaches about the relation between the final aim and means of His instruction. He distinctly decided the Hokekyo to be the highest authority on which all beings must depend and trust. In IV to IX he treats mainly of the problem between man and Buddha and the relations between the Hokekyo and all other Scriptures, with various allegories.

In the tenth chapter are shown the kinds of practice, the position of the Scripture, the value of the Scripture, the method of propagation, the opponents, the real Signification of Attainment of Buddhahood, etc. And the object person to this chapter is *Yakuō*, the Medicine-King. These ten chapters were sermonized on the Vulture Peak.

Chapter XI treats of the problem of the Stupa ; the twelfth chapter, " Devadatta," treats of the possibility of the attainment of Buddhahood by wicked people and especially by women. In the thirteenth chapter, Buddha teaches the positive method of propagation and prophesies the future. In the fourteenth chapter, negative methods of propagation and individual cultivation of moral character are taught. The former half ended here. In the fifteenth chapter, Buddha prepared to reveal the profound signification of His own personality, and for that purpose innumerable hosts of holy disciples were generated out of the earth. In the sixteenth chapter, Buddha proclaimed and revealed the truth to perfection. Chapters XVIII and XIX treat of the value and signification of religious life and the different kinds of conditions of believers. In Chapter XX the value and benefit of the positive method of propagation are taught under the name of *Fukyo*. In Chapter XXI Buddha entrusted all his precious mysteries to Honge Jogyo, and He performed ten great miracles which symbolized the unity of the future religions. In Chapter XXII, Buddha entrusted the task of propagation to all Bodohisattovas in general. These chapters were preached in heaven, which heaven must of course be understood in accordance with philosophical ideas. Thus, the pulpits in heaven ended and returned to the earth.

The last chapter of the first preaching on the earth had Yakuō, Medicine-King, as its object person. Now, the later sermons on the earth begin anew and, in the twenty-third chapter, Yakuō is again the object person, evidently having some reference to the signification of the system of this Scripture.

From XXIII to XXVIII, all sorts of beings vow to protect the righteousness of the Scripture and the Keepers in the future. Thus ends the Hokekyo.

N.B.—Readers of Kern's translation must be careful about the classifyings of chapters. Kumaraju's translation is composed of twenty-eight chapters, the eleventh being entitled " The Stupa " and the twelfth " The Devadatta." But the extant Sanscrit texts combine these two. Consequently, after Chapter XI, Kuma-

raju's translation has one more number than Kern's
translation and the Sanscrit texts.

8. BUDDHA'S PROPHECY

Buddha Shakamuni has already revealed his perfect
idea of truth as the Myohorengekyo. Thereupon He
wished to expand and continue His creative activities
and benevolence even into the far future, so here we
must not neglect Chapter XI, entitled " The Apparition
of the Heavenly Shrine."

This chapter describes the appearance in heaven of
a great and magnificent shrine decorated with the
seven kinds of precious jewels, just in the very front
of Shakamuni who was in the pulpit. And then a
voice was heard from within the shrine in admiration
of Shakamuni's revelation of Truth. The voice spoke
as follows, by the Buddha *Taho* (Skt. Prabhūta-
Satona, i.e. the Buddha of Accumulated Treasures) :

" Excellent, excellent, Lord Shakamuni ! Thou
hast well expounded this Dharmaparyaya of the Lotus
of the True Law. So it is, Lord; so it is, Sugata."

Lord Shakamuni then darted a bright ray from his
brow toward the ten directions of space, whence a
great multitude of Bodohisattovas happened to be
coming to see Lord Shakamuni, and they all assembled
in this world. But this world was too small to let
them sit down together, notwithstanding that they
formed a diminutive part of the magnificent bodies
of Lord Shakamuni. Kern's translation runs thus :

" At that moment the whole sphere was replete
with Tathagatas, but the beings produced from the

proper body of the Lord Shakamuni had not yet arrived, not even from a single point of the horizon."

Therefore, Shakamuni enlarged this world to a vast one in the eight directions and purified it, thus He enlarged and purified the world three times. But we cannot help wondering, how it was done by Buddha Shakamuni who had become Buddha only forty years earlier. One of the most important problems lies here, namely His eternal personality, which was suggested in the above story and will be properly brought to light in Chapter XVI. But Buddha's great hint was lost upon them so far as this Chapter XI is concerned.

Thus, the Buddha Taho bore testimony to the authenticity of Shakamuni's preachings. In the course of this dramatic manifestation the Stupa was opened in the heavens, surrounded by many Bodohisattovas and holy things. As soon as the shrine was opened the Buddha Taho invited Shakamuni to enter, and the two of them sat side by side in the Stupa in the heavens. Let us explain by the contextual quotation.

" And in the minds of those four classes of the assembly rose this thought ; We are far off from the two Tathagatas ; therefore let us also, through the power of Tathagata, rise up to the sky. As the Lord apprehended in his mind what was going on in the minds of those four classes as meteors in the sky. Thereupon the Lord Shakamuni, the Tathagata, addressed the four classes ; who amongst you, monks, will endeavour to expound this Dharmaparyaya of the Lotus of the True Law in this Saha world ? The fatal term, the time (of death), is now at hand ; the Tathagata longs for complete extinction, monks, after entrusting to you this Dharmaparyaya of the Lotus of the True Law " (Kern, pp. 237–8 ; Yamakawa, pp. 354–5).

The Koku-e, Preachings in Heaven, begin thus, as has been previously mentioned. This is simply the desire to testify to the truth of the Shakumon and bring in the Honmon afterwards. All Bodohisattovas were encouraged by this admonition of Buddha Shakamuni. They rose from their seats and strove in emulation for permission to be entrusted with the propaganda of the Hokekyo in the future. Readers will find these things fully set out in Chapters XI to XIV.

We must, however, mention the stanzas in Chapter XIII, in which Buddha prophesied all things about Honge Jogyo, who was entrusted with all the rights and mission of the propagation of the Sutra in the future. Let us have an idea of what the Scripture tells :

" O exalted One ! be little anxious for us !
After Thy great decease,
In the evil ages full of fears and dangers,
We shall proclaim the supreme Scripture.

There will then surely be malignant men,
And they will deride us and abuse us,
Lay upon us with weapons and sticks.
All these things we shall bear with endurance and persever-
ance.

In the Latter Days there will be monks,
Who, being malicious and crooked in mind,
Will pretend to have attained what is not really attained,
And their minds will be full of vain pride.

There will be those who dwell in forests (Āranyaka)
Living in tranquility and wearing the regular robes ;
They pretend to practise the true monastic life,
And despise all other men.

They will preach to laymen,
Simply for the sake of fame and profit ;
And yet they will be revered by the people,
As if they were endowed with the six supernormal powers.

In the evil days of the ages full of turbulence
There will be many fears and dangers ;
There will be men possessed by devils,
And they will abuse and insult us.

By revering Buddha and putting confidence in him,
And by wearing the armour of forbearance,
We shall endure all these perils,
For the sake of proclaiming this Scripture.

We shall never be fearful in sacrificing our bodily life,
But always regard the true Way as the highest cause ;
And thus we shall throughout all coming days,
Stand for the Cause committed to us by Buddha.

O Exalted One ! Thou may'st be assured,
Even when the vicious monks of the turbulent ages,
Being ignorant of the sermons preached by Buddha,
According to his tactful method,

Shall revile and rebuke us ;
And we be repeatedly driven out of our abodes,
And kept away from our sanctuaries,
Even then, we shall endure all these injuries,
By keeping ourselves to Buddha's decrees.

In whatsoever cities or villages,
There may be any who would seek the Truth,
Thither we shall surely go
And preach the Truth entrusted to us by Thee.

We are Thy messengers, O exalted One !
We have nothing to fear from any people,
We shall proclaim the Truth, to deserve Thy Commission
Thou may'st be assured and rest secure.

Now we take these vows in Thy presence,
And in the presence of all Buddhas
Who have come from the ten quarters.
May'st Thou, O Buddha, know our intention and determi-
nation ! "

(Yamakawa, pp. 389–93; Kern, pp. 259–61).[1]

These stanzas prophesied Honge Jogyo's activity in the days of the Latter Law. At the beginning of Chapter XV, " Issuing-out-of-the-Earth," these Bodohisattovas begged that they might preach Buddha's True Law in the future, but, contrary to expectation, Buddha endeavoured to dissuade them therefrom. They were utterly surprised. At that very moment, the innumerable Bodohisattovas, following the four leaders whose senior was named Visista-Cāritra, Honge Jogyo, appeared in quick succession out of the Earth, but nobody knew, even from one of themselves, what sort of Bodohisattovas they were. The general astonishment increased more and more ; at last, Bodohisattova *Miroku* (Skt. Maitreya), as the representative, asked Buddha, " Who are these Bodohisattovas who have just appeared out of the Earth ? None of us, not even I, know who they are." Then the answer came they were none other than His disciples from eternity, but the answer was *ignotum per ignotius* for them. So Miroku put his question to Buddha again with an allegory. ·

[1] This is taken from Anesaki's incomplete translation in: "Nichiren, the Buddhist Prophet," pp. 39–41.

" How, then, O Lord, has the Tathagata, after he left, when a prince royal, Kapilavastu, the town of Shakas, arrived at supreme, perfect enlightenment, not far from the town of Gaya, somewhat more than forty years since, O Lord ? How then has the Lord, the Tathagata, within so short a lapse of time, been able to perform the endless task of a Tathagata, the energy of a Tathagata ? How has the Tathagata, within so short a time, been able to rouse and bring to maturity for supreme, perfect enlightenment this host of Bodohisattovas, a multitude so great that it would be impossible to count the whole of it, even if one were to continue counting for hundred thousands of myriads of Kotis of Æons ? These Bodohisattovas, so innumerable, O Lord, so countless, having long followed a spiritual course of life and planted roots of goodness under many hundred thousands of Buddhas, have in the course of many hundred thousands of Æons become finally ripe.

" It is just as if some man, young and youthful, a young man with black hair and in the prime of youth, twenty-five years of age, would represent centenarians as his sons, and say : ' Here, young men of good family, you see my sons ; ' and if those centenarians would declare : ' This is the father who begot us.' Now, Lord, the speech of that man would be incredible, hard to be believed by the public. It is the same case with the Tathagata, who but lately has arrived at supreme, perfect enlightenment, and with these Bodohisattovas Mahasattovas, so immense in number, who for many hundred thousand myriads of Kotis of Æons, having observed a spiritual course of life, have long since come to certainty in regard to Tathagata-Knowledge ; who are able to plunge in and again rise from the hundred thousand sorts of meditation ; who are adepts at the preparatories to noble transcendent wisdom, have accomplished the preparatories to noble transcendent wisdom ; who are clever on the Buddha-ground, able in the (ecclesiastical) Council and in Tathagata duties ; who are the wonder and admiration of the world ; who are possessed of great vigour, strength, and power. And the Lord says : From the very beginning have I roused, brought to maturity, fully developed them to be fit for this Bodohisattova position. It is I who have displayed this energy and vigour after arriving at supreme, perfect enlightenment. But, O Lord, how can we have faith in the words of the Tathagata, when he says : The Tathagata speaks infallible truth ? The Tathagata must know that the Bodohisattovas who have newly entered the vehicle are apt to fall into doubt on this head ; after the extinction of the Tathagata those who hear this Dharmaparyaya will not accept, not believe, not trust it. Hence, O Lord, they will design acts tending to the ruin of the law. Therefore, O Lord, deign to explain to us this matter, that we may be free from perplexity, and that the Bodohisattovas who in future shall hear it, be they young men of good family or young ladies, may not fall into doubt " (Kern, pp. 294–6 ; Yamakawa, pp. 445–9).

Therefore, the Buddha Shakamuni was obliged to explain the matter to bring it down to their comprehension. Chapter XVI, " Duration of the Life of the Tathagata," was intended to solve this serious problem and to reveal the everlasting life of Buddha. According to the doctrine in the sixteenth chapter, the Buddha Shakamuni, who was born in India and was going to die, is only a manifestation for the sake of convenience and for the benefit of salvation. Shakamuni's Buddhahood is neither an acquisition since He appeared in India nor in the course of births and deaths, but He always lives and works through all eternity. He is the One who embodies the cosmic Truth throughout eternity and the nature of the endurance of the Truth. So Buddha says in the verses in the sixteenth chapter :

" Innumerable Æons have rolled by
 Since I have attained Buddhahood ;
 And I have been constantly preaching laws ever since
 Thereby leading innumerable people in the path of Buddha."

(Yamakawa, pp. 468–9 ; Kern, 307).

He, therefore, had explained Himself even in Chapter III as follows :

" Now, this threefold world is my realm wholly,
 All beings therein are my children,
 Though this place is full of suffering and tribulation
 I am the sole One who can save people in the world."

(Yamakawa, p. 139 ; Kern, p. 88).

Buddha ought naturally to have Honge Jogyo in order to expand and expound His eternal personality. And, now, having got His proper inheritor, He must entrust to him all His possessions and rights. In Chapter XXI, " Mysterious Powers of Tathagata," Buddha revealed ten apocalyptic miracles which contain great matters for the future civilized world.

And afterwards He entrusted everything to Honge Jogyo.

" In this Dharmaparyaya, *I have succinctly taught*[1] all Buddha-laws (or Buddha qualities), all the superiority, all the mystery, all the profound conditions of the Buddhas. Therefore, young men of good family, this Dharmaparyaya shall be made known, read, written, meditated, expounded, studied or collected into a volume ; be it in a monastery or at home, in the wilderness or in a town, at the foot of a tree or in a palace, in a building or in a cavern, on that spot one should erect a shrine in dedication to the Tathagata. For such a spot must be regarded as a terrace of enlightenment ; such a spot must be regarded as one where all Tathagatas have arrived at supreme, perfect enlightenment ; on that spot have all Tathagatas moved forward the wheel of the law ; on that spot one may hold that all Tathagatas have reached complete extinction."

Further, Buddha spoke about Honge Jogyo's character, he says :

" He who *keeps* this Sutra, the veritable law, will fathom the mystery of the highest man ; will soon comprehend what truth it was that was arrived at on the terrace of enlightenment.

" The quickness of his apprehension will be unlimited ;

---

[1] Kern, p. 367. In the Myohorengekyo translation, Kern's " *I have succinctly taught* " runs as follows : " *Summing up the salient points*, in this Scripture, I have preached, revealed and taught all Buddha's Laws, etc." This is much more correct than Kern's, consequently than the original from a doctrinal point of view. Yamakawa, p. 563.

like the wind he will nowhere meet impediments ; he knows the purport and interpretation of the law, he who keeps this exalted Sutra.

" He will, after some reflection, always find out the connection of the Sutras spoken by the leaders ; even after the complete extinction of the leader he will grasp the real meaning of the Sutras.

" He resembles the moon and the sun ; he illuminates all around him, and while roaming the earth in different directions he rouses many Bodohisattovas " (Kern, p. 369).

The latter part of the same verses in the Myo-horengekyo runs as follows :

" He will, after the complete extinction of Tathagata, know the origin and orders, and he will preach the law as it is according to the real signification of Buddha's Scriptures. Just as the light of *the sun* and moon does shine into darkness and dimness on the earth, so does *this person* expel ignorance (or gloom) from all beings."

It must be noted firstly that the term " keep," which is used in the above quotation, means not only mouth and mind, but the reading of the Hokekyo with body and life or flesh and blood, i.e. the practice. The Japanese technical term " Juji " is the equivalent. And secondly, that by " the Sun," as above, and " the lotus " in the following eulogy of Honge Jogyo's character : " Those who have well learned the way of Bodohisattovas purify themselves from the evil law of the world, just as the lotus does in the water " (Yamakawa, p. 450 ; Kern, p. 296), Nichiren was suggested, and got his name " Nichiren " when he left *Hiei monastery* and made his first denouncement at *Kiyosumi* in 1253 ; for " *Nichi* " means " *the Sun* " and " *ren* " means " *the lotus.*"

Thus, the Scripture and Buddha Himself were entrusted to Honge Jogyo. But after this, in Chapter XXII (Kern, XXVII, The Period), Buddha entrusted this mission to all ordinal Bodohisattovas in general, somewhat as follows :

" Into your hands, young men of good family, I transfer and transmit, entrust and deposit this supreme and perfect enlightenment attained by me after hundred thousands of myriads of Kotis of incalculable Æons " (Kern, p. 440 ; Yamakawa, p. 569).

However they were entrusted, they are nothing but the Bodohisattovas of *Shakke*. So they cannot have power to propagate this Law. Therefore Buddha instructed them in regard to this point as follows :

" And if there are unbelieving persons, guide and instruct them with the help of other kinds of Tathagata's significant laws."

" *Significant laws* " means all the other laws besides the Hokekyo. This idea is important to explain Tendai's and Dengyo's standpoints in the History of Buddhism from a doctrinal point of view.

In Kern's translation, the above lines are to the following effect : " And as to unbelieving persons, rouse them to accept this law."

And then :

" Thereupon, the Lord Shakamuni, the Tathagata, etc., dismissed all those Tathagatas, etc., who had

E

come to the gathering from other worlds, and wished them a happy existence, with the words : May the Tathagatas, etc., live happy. Then he restored the Stupa of precious substances to the Lord Prabhutaratna, the Tathagatas, etc., to its place, and wished him also a happy existence " (Kern, p. 441 ; Yamakawa, p. 572).

Thus ended the Preaching in Heaven and " Go-Ryozen-e," the concluding portion follows, wherein all Buddhas and Bodohisattovas were entrusted with the propagation of these Scriptures in the future. The Buddha Taho listened to these six chapters as the Buddha of attestation in the Stupa which has just been closed.

The remaining six chapters treat of the vow of the Bodohisattovas for the propagation of the Scriptures and for the protection of the keepers of the Scriptures. Now, we have stated the main story of the Hokekyo.

On the other hand, we must not neglect another scripture, " *The Daishukkyo* " (Skt. Mahā-Sannipātā), in which Buddha Shakamuni prophesied another thing. According to that scripture, Buddha divided the age after His Death into " Three Ages and Five Epochs," and prophesied in detail concerning them. The Three Ages are : the Right-Law Age (Jap. Shŏ-bŏ) for 1000 years after Buddha's extinction, and the Copied- (or Fanciful-) Law Age (Jap. Zŏ-bŏ) for the next 1000 years after the preceding, and the Latter-Law Age (Jap. Mappo) for the 10,000 years after the above two ages.

In the Right-Law Age, the Teachings (Kyo), Practices (Gyo) and Awakenings or Enlightenments

(Sho or Satori) are fulfilled entirely by the people. In the Copied-Law Age, people still have Buddha's Teachings and Practices with very occasional Awakenings, and everything is formalized. And in the Latter-Law Age, Buddha's Teachings alone remain ; in other words, the Scriptures and doctrines exist, but people merely regard them as an amusement and care nothing for Practices and Awakenings. This is the most degenerate Age.

Secondly, the " Five Epochs " or the " Fivefold Five Hundred Epochs," are the narrow divisions of the Three Ages. It is shown as under :

The first, the rigid epoch of Salvation or Emancipation.
The second, the rigid epoch of Meditation.
The third, the rigid epoch of Much-Reading and Hearing.
The fourth, the rigid epoch of Much-Making of Temples and Images.
The fifth, the rigid epoch of Battles and Wars.

If that be the prophecy, what are the effects ? According to Nichiren's view (Works, p. 112), it is pretty certain that Ānanda, Sānakavāsa, Puṇyaya śas and many others appeared and kept Buddhism during the first five hundred years. Much effective result was evident in this epoch as shown by the name Under Much Influence of Hinayana Buddhism. In the second epoch, Aśvaghoṣa, Nāgārjunā, Deva, Vasuvandhu, etc., appeared in India and Hinayana Buddhism gradually gave place to Mahayana Buddhism. Introspective or philosophical thinking was welcomed by the people, but all the same Buddhism had been divided into numerous Schools and began to wane since Hinduism arose. Thus, Buddhism was leaving India by degrees and was being transferred from India to China. In the third epoch it was predominant in China. Many Scriptures were translated during about three hundred years, from the *Go-Kwan Dynasty* to the dynasty of *Shin*, ever since Buddhism came to China.

Shiken, Kumaraju, Kakuken, Donmushin, Hokken, Jiku no Hōgō, Bodairushi (Bodohiruci), *Shintai* (Paramārtha) were the authorities among the translators. *Ekwan, Tendai, Eshi*, etc., were great Buddhist philosophers, and numerous works besides translations were published in those days. Buddhist philosophy was also systematized by Tendai, as I have already mentioned. Thus, this epoch was approaching the Hokekyo centric age. Moreover, Buddhism again began to leave China for Japan about this time. In the fourth epoch, together with Buddhism, the value of formalism must be noticed, seeing that Buddha's prophecy is true. Quite suddenly splendid Buddhist fine art was evolving in the Dynasty of *Tow* in China, and in Japan also in the *Nara-Epoch* and *Heian-Epoch*, which we see in the vicinity of *Kyoto* and *Nara*. The Great Masters, *Kōbō* and Dengyo, have built the monasteries of the " *Kongōbuji* " of the former and of the " Hiei " of the latter.

During the Copied-Law Age, Much-Reading and Hearing, and Much-Making of Temples were thus being realized ; so the fourth epoch did not belie its allotted names. Dengyo roused the movement of the Hokekyo centric religion and established the Mahayana Holy Altar (or Holy See) on Hiei by the Emperor's permission. Since Buddhism was transferred to Japan, it had decayed in India and China and Korea ; on the other hand, all Buddhist schools, all the Scriptures, all the reference books and all theory saw their prime in Japan, and are still there in a perfect state of maintenance.

However, the fifth epoch has come. Many terrible wars are fought in this epoch, within and beyond the sphere of the religious world, just as the title sets forth. The famous battles among the temples by the monks in Japan were continued for over three hundred years. For instance, the battles between the Hiei monastery and the *Onjō* monastery ; the Hiei versus the *Mii*, the *Kōya*, the *Negoro*, etc. etc. These are the battles in the circle of Buddhists. The war of *Hogen* era ; that of *Heiji* era ; the wars between the clans *Genji* and *Heike* and the rebellion of *Shōkyū* era, etc., these are the battles in the fields of politics and war. And again, the war between *So* and *Kettan ;* the battles among *Kwa*, *Kin* and *So*, in China, as well as the expedition to Rome of Henry IV ; the Holy Wars ; *Butto's* invasion of Russia and his battle with the allied armies of Northern Europe and so forth. All these have occurred in the Fifth epoch. By no means, therefore, can we deny the fact of the loss of authority of religion. Therefore, Buddha says in the Daishukkyo :

" Buddhist religion will disappear and will lose its grace and power of reclamation during the Fifth epoch."

But, on the other hand, there is another prophecy with exactly the opposite view in the Hokekyo.

" . . . . that at the end of time, the last period, in the latter half of the millennium it may have course here in Gambudvipa and not be lost " (Kern, p. 391 ; cp. Yamakawa, pp. 593, 596, 671, etc.).

Nichiren, therefore, very often made mention of the fact ; we may cite an instance :

" Now, 200 years more have elapsed since the Day of the Latter-Law began, and it corresponds with the time ' Buddhist law will disappear ' as recorded in the Daishukkyo. If Buddha's prophecy be true, it is the time that battles and wars shall take place in the world. . . . Buddha's prophecy on this is true after all, just as the flow and ebb of the water of the Ocean keeps time. There is no doubt, therefore, that, for this reason, the great law of the Hokekyo will spread over Japan and the whole world after the time of the prophecy of the Daishukkyo " (Works, pp. 117–8 ; cp. *ibid.*, p. 581, pp. 332–4).

Buddha's prophecy for the future has ended thus. Nichiren says :

" Now, the time has reached the beginning of the Latter-Law Age. It corresponds with the day of the appearance of Jogyo, who has learned and practised with all purity the essence of the ' Duration of the Buddha's Life ' of the Honmon from all eternity " (Works, p. 542).

Nichiren convinced himself that he was Jogyo in consequence of his practices and by the realization of Buddha's prophecy. He announced, therefore, that he himself was the sole saviour in the Days of Latter-Law, and that he was the entrusted authority and the right one for the propagation of the Scripture. It is impossible to understand him without knowing about these statements, because he framed all his sayings and actions from this point of view. Let us diagrammatize the relation of " Three Ages and Five Epochs " between the development of doctrine, etc. (See p. 56.)

Nichiren thus asserts himself as Jogyo, but at the same time he interprets great Buddhist masters who did not propagate the Hokekyo, or at least did not do so with enthusiasm. He says :

" These great scholars and masters were not supposed to ignore the profound significance of the Hokekyo. But the time which was destined for the propagation of the Scripture had not yet arrived, besides it was the precious law which was not entrusted to them by Buddha Shakamuni, so they bore it in mind, but did not speak it. Sometimes it seemed that they spoke the Law as it were, but the true signification was latent " (Works, p. 542).

Nichiren discovered the four reasons, as he states in one of his letters : 1. They are unable to. 2. No capability. 3. Not entrusted by Buddha. 4. The time is not come (Works, p. 304).

9.   NICHIREN'S CRITIQUE OF BUDDHIST SECTS

A.   Method

According to the result of the Five Principles, Nichiren now cast his eyes on several Buddhist sects which were in their prime. He severely criticized

Three Ages						
1000 years of the Right-Law Age (Teachings Practice Deliverance)	The rigid period of Deliverance (500 years)	(The days of prosperity of Hinayanism)	Buddhist Criticism on (Brahamanism), etc.	Five periods within Buddha's prophecy	Nichiren's Reformation	
	The rigid period of Meditation (500 years)	(Rise of Mahayanism)	Mahayanist Criticism on Hinayanism			
1000 years of the Fanciful-Law Age. Teachings, (formal practices)	The rigid period of Much-Reading and Hearing. (500 years)	(The days of prosperity of Mahayanism)	Reciprocal Criticism on Mahayanism			
	The rigid period of Much-Making of temples and images (500 years).	(Rise of the Shakumon centric religion)	Criticism on general Mahayanism from the point of view of the Shakumon.			
10,000 years of the Latter-Law Age. (Teachings).	The rigid period of combatings (500 years)	(Rise of the Honmoncentric religion)	Criticism on general Mahayanism and on the Shakumon from the point of view of the Honmon.		Foundation of Nichiren-ism.	
	The ulterior period without Buddha's prophecy (all periods)	(Circulation of the Honmon centric religion)	Fall of general Buddhism. Rise of special Buddhism	posterity.		

Works, pp. 667–8, p. 278, p. 581. Satomi " New Study of Nichirenism," pp. 311–48. Works, pp. 100, 103, 506.

these with a firm conviction, as demonstrated by the Scriptures. In respect of criticism, he strictly adhered to the authority of the Scriptures and facts, and often advocated the " Four Laws " of the *Nehangyo* (Skt. Mahāparinirvāṇa-Sūtra). Buddha says in it :

" Those monks shall trust the Four Laws : What are the four ? Trust the Law, but not Man : Trust Signification of the Scriptures, but not mere words ; Trust wisdom, but not knowledge ; Trust the Perfect Scripture, but not the Scriptures in imperfection."

Nichiren believed faithfully in this instruction of Buddha and therefore he could not help attacking all Buddhist sects. His criticism can be divided into two classes, the one is a general criticism and the other a special one. He thoroughly investigated all the Scriptures and he began by classifying them according to their signification and to Buddha's words. When he came across the Muryogikyo, the prolegomena to the Hokekyo, he found the following words :

" I did not reveal the truth (in all my previous preachings) during more than the past forty years."

So he sought for Buddha's true teaching and attained the Truth of the Hokekyo. He also saw an express provision in the third chapter of the Scripture. It is somewhat as follows :

" Do not accept a single stanza from any other Scriptures " (Yamakawa, p. 154 ; cp. Kern, p. 96).

And again, in the same chapter, Buddha says :

" If a man will not believe this Scripture and will destroy and abuse it, this means the destruction of the Buddha-Seed in the whole world. . . . That man shall fall into the Nethermost Hell after death " (Yamakawa, pp. 146-7 ; Kern, p. 92).

Consequently Nichiren writes :

" All assurances about Attainment of Buddhahood in the pre-Hokekyo Scriptures are just like unto the stars and the moon in the water ; all assurances about Attainment of Buddhahood which were preached prior to the Hokekyo are just like unto shadows of bodies. If I criticize them from a point of view of the sixteenth chapter of the Hokekyo, all the assurances of Attainment of Buddhahood with pious imposition are mere words when they deviate from the wisdom of the Duration of Buddha's Life, the sixteenth chapter " (Works, p. 1301).

Let us cite another example :

" When they deviate from the Hokekyo, even though they should practice *all teachings with pious imposition* during innumerable years, they would fall into Hell one and all. This is not what I, Nichiren, say, but the rule determined by Buddha Shakamuni and Taho and all the Buddahs in the ten directions " (Works, pp. 957, 1313, 1333, 1364, 1137).

He, then, proclaimed most emphatically :

" All the sects are the radical way to Hell, while the Hokekyo is alone the truth in Buddhahood " (Works, p. 634).

But Nichiren by no means denies the relative value of the other Scriptures. He only contends that the

Hokekyo is the sole truth to attain Buddhahood, consequently he denied all other Scriptures on that point. Therefore he says :

" If believers of the other Scriptures would only adore the truth of the Hokekyo, they would acquire the Principle of the Mutual Participation. Then all other Scriptures would be the Hokekyo, and vice versa. The Hokekyo does not deviate from all Pious-imposition-Scriptures nor vice versa. This is what is called Mysterious Law. As soon as this understanding was brought about, reading the Hinayana Scriptures is equivalent to reading the Mahayana Scriptures and the Hokekyo " (Works, p. 1234).

Moreover, he says :

" You may judge everything in accordance with common sense unless it prevents the Path to Buddhahood " (Works, p. 822).

Consequently, Nichiren examined all the sects and denounced the four representative ones.

B.   *The Nenbuts Sect*

Nichiren attacked the Nenbuts Sect (*Jōdo*) primarily in order to bring about religious reformation. This sect was found addicted to the Easiest Practice, namely simple-hearted devotion to the Buddha Amita. This sect apparently took hold of the common people of that time. It denies all effects of any other kind of religious thinking and practice, because by these methods it is too difficult for people to attain Buddhahood. Therefore, *Honen*, the founder of the sect, completely abolished those methods and all the Buddhist Sacred Books. He then only needed to think of Amita's name and repeat it.

Nichiren denounced this sect for about eight main reasons. First of all, he noticed that this sect held with the Pious-imposition-Scriptures to which our notice has already been drawn (Works, pp. 1527–8). Secondly, Honen's proclamation, viz. " Leave, shut, neglect and cast away the Hokekyo " is the destruction of Buddha's True Teaching, which is prohibited as being the Fourteen Disparagements (Works, pp. 1527, 1431). Thirdly, this sect is an anachronistic one concerning time and capability (Works, pp. 1428–9). Fourthly, the sect is the traitor to Buddha Shakamuni, the founder of Buddhism and the Sole Lord of this Threefold world, for, instead of Shakamuni, Amita of the Western Paradise is worshipped as the sole saviour, but this, as a matter of course, contradicts the True Teaching of Buddhism (Works, pp. 1410–1). Fifthly, the Sacred Title of the Hokekyo is not a mere lemma of the book, but it is the essence of the truth and the seed of Buddha. It is pronounced vividly in Chapter XXI that All Buddhas could become Buddahs by conceiving the Essence, the Sacred Title of the Hokekyo. Therefore to abandon the Hokekyo is tantamount to deserting the original Seed of Buddha (Works, p. 1510). Sixthly, according to the seventh chapter of the Scripture, Amita's proper task consists in the propagation of the Hokekyo. Honen's proclamation is far from being Amita's true vow. The interpretation about Amita Buddha in the Pious-imposition-Scriptures is not the true revelation of Amita's character and vow (Works, p. 339).

Seventhly, the sect rejected the Hokekyo as being the Difficult Way, whereas the Easiest Practice is actually taught in several chapters of the Hokekyo. This is due to their ignorance of even the problems of the Easy and Difficult Ways of religious practice (Works, p. 1433). Eighthly, Amita Buddha, in short, is a production of the imagination with a view to educating. He does not exist at all. He is simply an emanated Buddha, solely from Buddha Shakamuni. The so-called Western Paradise wherein Amita rules, is also the land of fancy; nevertheless, this sect clings to a theory which was intended as temporary instruction by Buddha Shakamuni (Works, p. 1370).

Nichiren thought that the religious practice after this life is a mere fancy. So he says :

" The practice for a hundred years in the Western Paradise is inferior to that of a day in this impure world " (Works, p. 196).

Such a religion, without doubt, impairs the vitality of human life. For that reason, Nichiren dared to say without hesitation that " The Nenbuts Sect leads people to the Nethermost Hell."

C.   The Zen Sect

As one of the new Buddhist schools, the Zen Sect was being introduced into Japan at that time, and it was greatly welcomed by people, in particular by warriors, viz. the *Samurais*. The peculiarity of that sect consists in its method of meditation. It denies all external authorities, but concentrates the whole mind on the intuitive insight of the internal ego. It therefore denies all the Buddhist Scriptures, Buddha, system and school, and it takes pride in Self-assertion. Nichiren attacked this sect for several reasons. Let us consider a few of them.

Firstly, one day when Buddha Shakamuni was on the Vulture Peak, *Sikhin*, the King of the threefold world, gave a flower of lotus to Buddha, and Buddha fingered it with a smile, looking at all His disciples: but nobody could understand why; only Mahakā-śyapa understood the deep meaning of His deed. Then, Buddha confided the truth to him. It is said that the Zen Sect owes its origin to the above story. Nichiren, to begin with, queried this point which is too obscure a story to be accredited (Works, p. 1366). Secondly, the Zen School asserts that it exists independently of the Scriptures and of Buddha's preaching, and that it is the true religion from heart to heart. But it seemed to Nichiren a great contradiction, because all the Zennists read the Scriptures, and they count twenty-eight sages from the founder as their ancestral leaders in spite of their denunciation of the school and system (Works, pp. 1405–7; cf. pp. 1219, 217). Thirdly, they say that the Scriptures are just like fingers which indicate the moon; when the fingers indicate the moon, they are of no more use. Nichiren compared this thought with such a view as that parents are of no use after we are born, and he attacked them severely (Works, pp. 1367, 1560). Fourthly, they say that Buddha is nothing but our minds, we and Buddha are one and the same. Nichiren saw here the imitative adoption of Tendai's doctrine and saw also their over-estimation of the Ego, or rather he thought that their assertion was the effect of their confusion of the relation of the phenomenal Ego and the substantial Ego (Works, pp. 1367, 1560). Nichiren went on to criticize several points and he boldly denounced " The Zen Sect " as " The Devil."

D.   *The Shingon Sect*

The third attack of Nichiren was directed against the Shingon Sect, which was giving secularism to the people, and which at that time predominated at the Court and among the nobility. This sect is an occult and magistic mysticism and accepts any vulgar actions as holy ones without criticizing ; as an extreme instance, promiscuous sexual intercourse is approved as being holy practice. Such a thought under the authority of a religion caused Buddhist degeneration and derangement of the Court and the nation, and Nichiren thought that not only was it the cause of derangement, but also of the devastation of the right doctrine of Dengyo. At that time, the Shingon mysticism was being broadcasted into the people by Dengyo's followers from the Buddhist centre, the Hiei monastery. Hereupon, Nichiren attacked this sect by means of his most powerful oratory and letters in spite of all difficulties.

To have the Buddha *Dainichi* (Skt. Mahāvairocana) as the sole saviour is evidently traitorous to the founder of Buddhism, Shakamuni ; and not merely that, but it is just like having two Kings in the same country. This is the first reason of Nichiren's denouncement of this sect (Works, p. 1578). The Shingon Sect contends that the *Dainichikyo* (Skt.

Mahāvairocanābhisambodohi-Sūtra) is the King of all the Scriptures, but it seems to Nichiren to be a dogmatic assertion, and not the right opinion, which upholds the golden saying of the Buddha. That is his second reason (Works, pp. 1590–1). For the third, the fourth, and the fifth reasons and so on, he analysed the doctrine of the sect into several radical elements and criticized the sect with keen and minute technical method from a point of view of immanent critique (Works, pp. 1555–6, 1369, 1578, 1623–5).

Nichiren also pointed out many facts of derangement of social orders which were caused by the sect, and he indicated the Shokyu-War as a natural result of the influence of the Shingon Sect (Works, p. 1570). Thus, this sect was denounced by him as " The Cause of National ruin."

E.   The Rits Sect

When Buddhism was first introduced into Japan, the doctrine of Hinayanism and a few Hinayana sects were already founded there, but they were dependent on some of the Mahayana sects. As a result of natural selection, those Hinayana sects began to decrease after a short time, while one sect which was called " Rits " was regenerating. Excessive value was set on formalism and everything was enforced by monastic rules. This sect advocated the adjustment of everything of an external nature, and consequently only required individual cultivation. In other words, it means technically, the revival of the old Hinayana Commandments, hence rigorism and ritualism.

Of course, it was at one time advantageous in India for the people, but in Nichiren's days the nature of things was too complicated to advocate such simple moral external rules. Nay, from the doctrinal point of view of the Hokekyo it is useless and detrimental in the Days of the Latter Law. Buddhist Commandments in the Latter Days should be a deep and fervent vow for the systematic reconstruction of the world and self, not merely individual training. Nichiren, therefore, could not fail to protest against this sect also. He called the Rits Sect " Traitor to the country " (Works, pp. 364-5, 543-4, 324-5, 716-7, 201, 571, 543, etc.). His four main denouncements are called by Nichirenians " Four apophthegms." " Nenbuts (Amita Buddhism) leads people to the Nethermost Hell, Zen is the Devil, Shingon ruins the country and Rits is traitor to the country," thus the Four apophthegms are composed.

He, further, criticizes the Tendai Sect, which favoured the Shakumon from the point of view of the Honmon.

Three kinds of opponents arose and they at once persecuted him. However, his firm conviction, which was suggested by the Hokekyo, carried him among his opponents with his life at stake to proclaim himself the prophesied man. We will examine this point circumstantially in Chapter IV.

F

III

THE THREE GREAT SECRET LAWS

(Sandai Hiho)

1. Meaning

After mentioning his Five Critical Principles we must observe what the religion of Nichiren is. He must now establish his own religion as the natural result of his investigations. The Five Principles naturally guide his positive religion, " The Three Great Secret Laws."

The Three Great Secret Laws are the three aspects of his religion, and they emanated from the One Law which is indicated by the Sacred Title of the Hokekyo. Each of the Three is the independent principle on the one hand, and again each of them is the essential moment of the One Law on the other hand, that is to say something like Hegel's " *aufgehobenes Moment*."

It is the three aspects of reality in the sense of the observance of Law ; it is the three expressions of the principle of typical personality in the significance of Buddha ; it is the three principles of the modes of our lives in the significance of being. Let us reduce the three aspects, then it will be the One Law, and vice versa. From another point of view, the Sacred Title is the religious subject which indicates the Self-containing He. The Supreme Being of the three is the religious object in which the religious subject exists, in other words, it is the He which contains our Selves therein. The Holy See of the three is the concrete realization of the religion.

The Sacred Title is the law of awakening of the individual : the Holy See is the principle of idealization of the country, and the Supreme Being is the harmonious manifestation of the world.

2. THE SACRED TITLE (HONMON DAIMOKU)

The Problem of the religious subject

The title of the Hokekyo is " Myohorengekyo." But we must mention here that this title is neither a mere title of the Book nor a nominal expression. This, indeed, implies all the value of the Scripture and represents the truth of the Lotus. If the Sacred Title is taken as a mere nominal title it is simply book-worship when people utter " Namu-Myohorengekyo," " Adoration to Myohorengekyo." We cannot attain the true meaning without comprehending the title, for the Sacred Title is the essence of the Hokekyo. The Hokekyo is, indeed, an interpretation of the Sacred Title. That is why Nichiren refers to this point so often in his writings. He says :

" The so-called Namu-Myohorengekyo is not only the essence of the entire Buddhist Scriptures, but is the heart, the substance and the ultimatum of the Hokekyo " (Works, p. 726 ; see *ibid.*, p. 727).

He preferred the essence, the Sacred Title among the three divisions which are the " Essence," the " Most Important Portion " and the " Whole of the Scripture." He denied the value of any Scriptures considered only from a literary point of view. Therefore he says :

" Although there are characters and letters of the Hokekyo, they are not the medicine for human spiritual illness."

He rejected the usual methods of thinking, meditation, reading, researching until people realize the essential quality of religion. According to him, the essence of religion does not consist in such rational practice, but is implied in faith. The Sacred Title is, indeed, the very thing to which our faith must attain in order that we may reach the fulness of the truth. It is, of course, the title, but the title is the key to the contents. Therefore he says :

" The name (or appellation or title) is intrinsically justified in calling the thing, and the latter feels it is entitled in its turn to respond. This is the signification of the Sacred Title " (Works, p. 229).

According to Tendai, the Sacred Title implies five significations contained in his famous doctrine " The Five Profound Significations " as under :

1.   The Title.
2.   The Entity.
3.   The Principle.
4.   The Efficiency.
5.   The Doctrine.

These five, as a matter of course, are implied in the Sacred Title, for we cannot think of any contents without a title, just as nobody can think of Shakespeare without knowing his name. Nichiren, in this respect, took the Sacred Title as Buddha-Seed, in which all virtues are inherent. Therefore it is an absolute necessity for a man seeking the truth of Buddhism to attain it by dint of practice of the Sacred Title. So Nichiren says :

" In the fifth five hundredth period of the beginning of the Latter Law, man shall not believe absolutely the view, though it be Buddha's teaching, that a man can attain Buddhahood, even if he be estranged from the Sacred Title of the Hokekyo " (Works, pp. 601, 228–9, 727).

Because, all the letters, 69384 words of the Hokekyo are nothing but the definition of the Sacred Title, just as in the relation between medicine and the description of its virtues.

The Sacred Title is the essence of the Hokekyo as we have stated above ; it means at the same time, the essence of life. Buddha's cosmic life is " Myohorengekyo," " Wonderful, mysterious, perfect and right truth." It is equivalent to the " Real Suchness." Everything of the universe is therein contained. Nichiren says :

" . . . . Therefore the manifestation of cosmos is equivalent to the five words of Myohorengekyo " (Works, p. 684).

The Sacred Title is therefore the principle of our lives or essence of our nature, and further this Sacred Title is the name of life which is analysed into ten worlds, and synthetized into One Buddha Centric

Existence under the principle of the Mutual Participation. He writes in this respect as follows :

" . . . . Therefore, if one can perceive that it is not a mere title of the Book, but our substance, because Buddha named our substance and nature as ' Myohorengekyo,' then our own selves are equivalent to the Hokekyo : and we know that we are the Buddhas whose Three aspects of character are united into One ; because Buddha manifested our true substance in the Hokekyo " (Works, pp. 659–60 ; see *ibid.*, pp., 228, 341–2).

Nichiren thus taught the intuition for the real self by the law of the Sacred Title. As the result of it, he advocated " Namu-Myohorengekyo," that is adoration or devotion to the Perfect Truth of the Scripture. In this case, the uttering is one of the important practices comprising about five reasons (Satomi, " Nichiren's Religion and its Practices," Japanese, pp. 131–3) :

1.   Self intuition or reflection.
2.   Expression of ecstasy.
3.   Stimulation of continuous impression.
4.   Autohypnotism for inspiration.
5.   Manifestation of one's standard.

Uttering must probably be studied from the point of view of psychology of religion and philosophy of religion. Without doubt, it is static as far as the Sacred Title is concerned, with the mere idea or conception, but when it is uttered by the voice and is heard by the ear, then it will become a dynamic moment of religion. The Sacred Title is the promise between God and man. Buddha reveals all His things under the name of the Sacred Title, and beings can see Buddha in it ; thus Nichiren thought. When our absolute devotion for the Sacred Title is completed, we can enter into Buddha's wisdom, despite our ignorance. In other words, we can accept Buddha's true wisdom by virtue of faith, that is the absolute dependence on Him. Nichiren explained this faith as the joyful loyal submission. He describes it in an ingenious allegory :

" Hearken ! religious faith is simply just like the love of a wife for her husband or a husband's devotion to his wife, or I should say a parent's heart for his or her children or the yearning of a child after its mother " (Works, p. 736).

Thus, Nichiren understood the Sacred Title ; therefore he says :

" Cause and effect of Buddha's enlightenment are innate in the five words of Myohorengekyo. If we keep these five characters, Buddha transfers the fruits of that cause and effect to us in a natural way " (Works, p. 94).

In consequence thereof we must carefully note that the Sacred Title is a law which permits individuals to vow to exert themselves to attain Buddhahood. In other words, our allotted lives, at any rate, are imperfect lives, in which divine nature and hellish nature reside together. We must cultivate the divine nature throughout our lifetime. " *Namu* " therefore means a vow of constant effort for the Attainment of Buddhahood. He says :

" Wise and ignorant, all people equally shall utter *Namu-Myohorengekyo* and abstain from any other vow of the kind " (Works, p. 196).

And to this Nichiren particularly draws our attention, he says :

" There are two different significations of the Sacred Title between the ages of the Right and Copied Laws and the age of the Latter Law. In the age of the Right Law, Vasuvandhu and Nāgārjunā, etc., adored the Sacred Title which they had limited within their own practices. In the age of the Copied Law, *Nangaku* (or *Eshi*), Tendai, etc., worshipped and uttered the Sacred Title, but they did it for the sake of their own practices, and did not propagate it widely to other people. Such attitudes are nothing but metaphysical methods. The Sacred Title which is uttered by me, Nichiren, in the Days of the Latter Law, is totally different from their attitudes in the previous ages. It is a ' Namu-Myohorengekyo ' for the sake of our own practice and at the same time for the sake of the salvation of all beings " (Works, pp. 240–1).

According to him, the Sacred Title must be kept by every individual, and this individual must strive for the salvation of his environment. What he chiefly meant was the instruction of individuals by the Law of the Sacred Title.

Let us consider his doctrine on this point from the point of view of philosophy of religion. Nominalism and realism or substantialism are kept in harmony in this doctrine of the Sacred Title. In addition we see therein a possible solution of the problem of knowledge and faith. He held the value of faith in religion in high esteem, therefore he admonished the people to live in faith. So, he wrote to one of his disciples :

"The slight knowledge regarding Buddhism of some of my disciples proved their bane" (Works, p. 729).

Further, he says :

"Our knowledge brings no profit whatever. If one has sufficient knowledge to distinguish between hot and cold, one should explore wisdom" (Works, p. 1609).

However learned a man may be his knowledge is apt to lead him astray unless he grasps the fundamental wisdom which is different from knowledge. We cannot rejoice in religious happiness without faith. Therefore he says :

"One may make oneself a learned man or scholar, but it is of no avail if one goes to hell" (Works, p. 1358).

Thus, he recognized the superiority of faith, but he by no means depreciated knowledge. The essential nature of religion must be faith, but reason and the will, after conviction of faith, lead faith on to the right path. He says :

"Be diligent in practice and research, if these two became extinct, then Buddhist Law would have perished.   So strive for them and cultivate other people.   But in all circumstances, these are derived from faith and belief " (Works, p. 502).

Nichiren, moreover, intended to solve the problem of the relation between God and man.   If the evil is denied, then goodness must be denied as a matter of course.   There is no God outside of our lust, nor divine thing except our nature.   Because our nature is existence as a whole, as is shown in the doctrine of the Mutual Participation.   Therefore if our lust were annihilated divine nature would then also be non-existent.   From such a point of view he did not adopt Stoicism or asceticism, while on the other hand he did not admit secularism or vulgarism.   With regard to this, he asserted that we must spiritualize lust and instinct, but not exterminate them.

Lust will turn into divine power if we spiritualize it.   Let lust be divine power, let evil be goodness and let the wicked perform divine action :   therein Nichiren's thought lies.   Once he writes to Shijo Kingo, a warrior, as under :

" Even when in the act of sexual intercourse if one devoted oneself to the Sacred Title, lust would be supreme signification and ' Life and Death is Nirvana ' would be found in it " (Works, p. 853).

He writes again to him :

" Utter ' Namu-Myohorengekyo ' even while drinking wine in company with your wife.   Don't let the heart suffer, don't indulge in any pleasure.   Be happy to utter the Sacred Title when fortune favours you or during the time of misfortune. Is it not the enjoyment of your own faith of the Hokekyo ? '' (Works, p. 711).

Thus did he teach his disciples, with views which totally differ from the Hinayana Buddhists' view of Nirvana. Therefore such an excellent law of the Sacred Title was declared to Honge Jogyo from Buddha Shakamuni in the Hokekyo for the purpose of propaganda in the beginning of the Latter Law. Let us now cite his writings :

'' Japan and China, India, nay, the whole world wherein every individual, wise or ignorant, one and all must call on the name of the Sacred Title, Namu-Myohorengekyo. In consequence of the lack of propagation, nobody having kept this law during the last 2225 years since Buddha's Death, I, Nichiren, alone am unceasingly repeating Namu-Myohorengekyo, Namu-Myohorengekyo, etc. . . . Namu-Myohorengekyo shall last for ever beyond the coming ages of 10,000 years, all the broader and greater in proportion to the magnitude of the benevolence of myself, Nichiren.

'' This is my merit that destined me to open the blind eyes of all beings in Japan (and in the world) by cutting off the way of communication to the Nethermost Hell. This merit is beyond those of Dengyo and Tendai, and it has an advantage over those of Nāgārjunā and Kāśyapa. Religious austerities (or practice) in the Paradise for a hundred years long are inferior to an accumulation of merit for a day in this impure world. Hearken ! all the propagation during the last two thousand years of the Right Law and the Copied

Law is inferior to that of a twinkling of an eye in the Latter Days, is it not ?

" All this superiority is not due to me, that is to say to Nichiren's wisdom, but to the changes of the times. Flowers bloom in spring, fruits ripen into maturity in autumn ; it is hot in summer and it is cold in winter. Are these not with the changes of the seasons ? " (Works, pp. 195–6 ; paragraphs of " An Essay in token of Gratitude " (to Nichiren's previous old master)).

According to the principle of Mutual Participation, all natures are inherent in our mind *a priori*, in other words, from God-nature to Satan-nature inhere in us. Therefore even the Buddha or God has quite naturally an evil nature or hellish mind ; Buddha is Buddha because He cultivated Himself and He enlightened all hellish natures and made them refined. So also can He redeem evil-natured people. If there is no element of Satan or hell or evil or that sort of thing in God or Buddha, He is a mere spiritual cripple. How can He redeem evil natures ? The conception of Sin must not be dramatized by mythology. Sin co-exists with divine nature in man and in God. But the difference between man and God depends on their effect for the enlightenment of natures. Thus, if we awake in our valuable nature and realize that its value continues everlastingly, in other words, from moment to eternity, from man to God, then we can recognize the true significance of lives. The doctrine of the Sacred Title is shown thus briefly.

3. THE SUPREME BEING (HONMON HONZON)

The Problem of the religious object

The Sacred Title was treated as the problem of a religious subject while the Supreme Being is going to be treated as a problem of a religious object. Every religion has its object for worship. In Nichirenism, with regard to this point, what kind of object is given ?

First of all, we must know the meaning of the Supreme Being itself. Three meanings were ascribed to the Supreme Being in Nichirenism. Originally, the word *Honzon* was a compound noun which can be divided into *Hon* and *Son* (Zon is an euphonical change). *Hon* means Origin and *Son* means augustness or supremacy. The innate supreme substance is the first definition, the second is the radical adoration, and the third is the genuine or natural respect. All these are slightly different expressions of the Supreme Being and its aspects.

There are two kinds of Supreme Beings in general. The one has the abstract principle as its religious object, while the other has a concrete idea of personality or person itself as its object of worship. In this connection, Nichiren has both simultaneously. According to him, Buddha Shakamuni is the only saviour in this world, therefore we must have Him as our object of religious worship. The following quotation demonstrates it :

" Worship, in Japan and the world, the Buddha

Shakamuni, the revealer of the Honmon of the Hokekyo, as the Supreme Being " (Works, p. 195).

On the other hand, he says :

" You shall have the Sacred Title of the Hokekyo as the Supreme Being " (Works, p. 348).

Thus, he founded two kinds of the Supreme Being, the object of worship. In other words, these are the Buddha centric Supreme Being and the Law centric one. And these two are united by him in his most important essay which is entitled " Spiritual Introspection of the Supreme Being," according to which the Buddha could attain Buddhahood by the virtue of His apprehension of the universal truth, without which a Buddha is impossible. The Buddha made Himself a Buddha by mastering the perfect truth of cosmos and by its actual realization. From that point of view it can be said that a personal Buddha is secondary if He is compared with the truth itself, on account of the truth being the mother of enlightenment and comprehension. But again, even if there exist such a splendid truth, it will be nothing, or a mere abstract conception at most, unless life be well comprehended and embodied. The Buddha Shakamuni is, indeed, the Sole Tathagata of the perfect truth. The enigma of the truth was enlightened and revealed by Him. Without Buddha's preaching the truth could not be revealed. In that sense, the Buddha made it possible for the abstract truth to become an actual one. Therefore, the Buddha and the truth cannot be separated as far as they are connected with this actual universe. Moreover, there are many conceptions of the Buddha, for instance, the Threefold personality (Skt. Trikāya), viz. the Body of truth (Dharmakāya), the Body of Wisdom (Sambhogakāya), the Body of phenomenal person (Nirmaṇakāya). These three attributes of Buddha's personality must be kept in harmony consistently. Moreover, as far as the contents of the Supreme Being are the universe, or as long as the Supreme Being is for human beings, the relation between the human nature and Buddha Nature must be solved.

The theory of the Tenfold Suchness in the Hokekyo, as we have mentioned already, guides the principle of the Mutual Participation. According to it, all beings have all the natures and tendencies of their various personal characters innately. Real Suchness, the truth of the universe, exists in such a phenomenon. Reality and phenomena are inseparable. But if there is no one who keeps the truth, then the truth or the law is equal to nothing. However high and sublime the Supreme Being may be, if we ourselves do not enter the ideal of it, and do not realize in our own lives its principle and form, it is just an idol and our existence worthless.

Therefore, all the beings, Buddha and man, saint and layman, must be united under the fundamental primeval virtues of the supreme principle of our lives. Animals, plants, human beings and all deities shall be harmonized into a unity. Nichiren treated plants and animals in reference to the problem of Attainment of Buddhahood as well as mankind (Works, " On the Attainment of Buddhahood of plants," p. 1293). He diagrammatized this union of the world at *Sado* during his exile there, and

systematized the theory of the Supreme Being in the
" Spiritual Introspection of the Supreme Being."
Let us cite a paragraph of his writing :

" The august appearance and condition of the
Supreme Being are thus : the Heavenly Shrine (Stupa)
is flying in heaven over this world of the Primeval
Master (Shakamuni). The Buddhas Shakamuni and
Taho are sitting side by side and also the four Bodo-
hisattovas, Jogyo, etc., are standing by the Buddha
Shakamuni as His attendants on either side of the
Sacred Title which is visible in the Shrine.

" *Monju* (Skt. Manjuśri) and Miroku, etc., as the
followers of the four Bodohisattovas, Jogyo, etc., take
the humbler seats, whereas the other innumerable
Bodohisattovas sit on the ground like unto people
looking up at the courtiers gathered round the throne.
Moreover, all the Buddhas who came from the ten
directions are on the earth in order to indicate the
local realms of the local Buddhas. Such a splendid
Supreme Being was not realized during Buddha
Shakamuni's days prior to the Hokekyo, even in the
Hokekyo, it was revealed only during the eight chapters
from XV to XXII " (Works, p. 95).

For all beings, gods and men, animals and plants,
spirits and demons, he gave the right position in the
Supreme Being, the Circle or the Mandala. All of
them, without exception, are surrounding the Sacred
Title of the centre, in other words, all the beings from
Buddha to Hell devoted themselves to the highest
truth of the Sacred Title. The Sacred Title is nothing
but the Buddha Shakamuni's true name, as well as
it is our own inherent nature. Realization of true self

through the Sacred Title according to the principle of the Mutual Participation is thus taught. Man or Buddha or God in the highest possible sense can be seen here with the true significance of life. Let us cite one more instance :

" How marvellous that, now, I, Nichiren, myself, at the termination of 200 years since the Latter Age began, represented the Great Maṇḍala as the flag of the propagation of the Hokekyo, which Maṇḍala could not be manifested even by Great Masters such as *Ryūju* (Skt. Nāgārjunā), *Tenjin* (Skt. Vasuvandhu), Tendai and Myoraku.

" However this is in no manner, my, Nichiren's, own invention, but it is proved by the Buddha Shakamuni and all the distributive Buddhas in the Heavenly Shrine. The Sacred Title, therefore, is hoisted in the centre and the Four Great Demon Kings (Japanese : *Shidai-Ten-no* who guard the world against) *Ashura* (Skt. Asura) take seats at the four corners in the Heavenly Shrine, the Buddhas Shakamuni and Taho and the Four Primeval Bodohisattovas (Honge Jogyo, etc.) stand abreast, *Fugen* (Samanta Bhadra), Monju, *Sharihots*, *Mokuren*, etc., take the humbler seats, the gods of the Sun and Moon, the King of Mara of the sixth *Devaloka*, the Serpent King and *Ashura* also join the body, moreover *Hudo* and *Aizen* are seated in the direction of south and north, atrocious Devadatta, the folly serpent maid, the mother of demons, Ten wives and daughters of the devils (Japanese : *Kishimojin*, Skt. Rākchasa) who make attempts on human life ; then the Sungoddess and God of Hachiman, both of the genius of Japan ; the gods of heaven

G

and earth, all kinds of deities, gods-in-nature are present ; how much more gods-in-themselves.   In Chapter XI it says :

" As the Lord apprehended in his mind what was going on in the minds of those four classes of the assembly, he instantly by magic power, established the four classes as meteors in the sky, etc. (Kern, p. 237 ; Yamakawa, p. 355).   These Buddhas, Bodo-hisattovas and great sages and all other beings, *Two worlds and Eight kinds* (i.e. all kinds) *of beings* who were present since the Introductory chapter of the Scripture, altogether, without exception, live in this Supreme Being, and all of them realize their innate value of personality under the brilliant light of the Five Characters of Myo-ho-ren-ge-Kyo.   Such is the Supreme Being " (Works, pp. 721, 722).

Keeping this in view it will be easy to understand that Nichiren's idea consisted in " *Coincidencia oppositorum* " and " Synthetic union."   According to him, all beings on the one side are a mass of lust, but nevertheless they are, on the other side, Buddha in nature or Buddha in substance.   Therefore if they would self-awaken to their true value and strain every nerve to get near their intrinsic Buddhahood, significant lives would be established.   For that reason he divided the Buddha into two kinds, viz. Buddha-in-Nature and Buddha-in-Realization.   The former corresponds to normal man and the latter means Buddha himself.   Besides, all beings from the Buddha to Hell or from man to all lower animate creatures are united in the highest principle, that is to say, Myohorengekyo.   Thus, this Mandala is, indeed, the real form of the Real Suchness or the world or self or the class harmonization. He, therefore, strongly advocated this Supreme Being in the absolute sense. He writes on the right side of the Supreme Being as under :

" This is the Great Maṇḍala which has never before appeared in this world during these two thousand two hundred and twenty years since Buddha's Decease."

On the left side is written :

" Having been condemned to die on the twelfth day of the ninth month, in the eighth year of Bunn-nei, but as I had, instead, been exiled later on to the distant Isle of Sado, on the eighth day of the seventh month, in the tenth year of the same, I, Nichiren, make this representation for the first time."

Thus Nichiren made the Supreme Being in a perfectly graphical method, which is much more effective than the ordinal Buddha's image or Buddha's picture or an abstract heaven. In this representation we can see that he treats several forms of worship under the principle of unity as under :

Dendolatry in the lotus, theriolatry in the serpent, demon-worship in the Mother of demons, great-man-worship in Tendai, etc., King-worship in Ajase, God-man-worship in Shakamuni, iconolatry in the Four Great Devas, racial-god-worship in the Sungoddess of Japan, national-god-worship in Hachiman of Japan, and ancestor-worship in ancestors, etc. etc.

Of course, all of them are united together by the principle of Myohorengekyo. We can identify ourselves with Buddha Himself if we truly awake and strictly practise the Attainment of Buddhahood. So Nichiren says :

" *The Heritage of the Sole Great Thing Concerning Life and Death* can be understood in the utterance of the Sacred Title, with the conviction that Buddha Shakamuni, who has attained Buddhahood from eternity, the Hokekyo and all beings, these three are but one " (Works, p. 677).

The interpretation of this doctrine has not yet been fully given, but we cannot expect to succeed in a technical explanation in this book, so we shall, for the present, examine a few problems concerning this thought.

There are two tendencies about the conception of God which must be noticed. The one is pantheism and the other is monotheism. Pantheism identifies God in nature, or looks upon Nature as partial appearances of the sole and absolute God. It shows immanency of God in opposition to deism. The Eleatics, Xenophanes, Parmenides, etc., advocated this theory in an early age, and Bruno, Spinoza, Fichte, Schelling, Hegel, Schleiermacher, Hartmann, Wundt, Lotze, etc., conceived this thought also. Spinoza is a pioneer of this thought in the modern age and his famous words " *Deus sive natura* " (God is nature) are quoted as the motto of pantheism.

Pantheistic thought in the history of religion germinated mainly among Aryan races and, according to Tiele, what is called theanthropic religion. Pantheism, as a rule, has a great system and a great ideal, and gives us not only a sensitive satisfaction, but likewise a rational one. But in pantheism there is no union in its vast system, and so it is very difficult to fix the religious object which is the object of our sentiment. Therefore religious practice can hardly be the outcome of it. If we look upon the universe or nature as a religious object there is, indeed, no religious object. Or if we consider our slight efforts of daily life as divine acts or religious practice, it is equal to having no religious practice at all. To make such pantheistic thought possible a deistic thought or an atheistic colour or maybe a polytheistic idea must be adduced.

On the other hand, monotheism has the One God who created this world from another world. The nature of God in monotheism is quite different from that of polytheistic gods. God is transcendent and we cannot mix up God and the universe. God and the world are totally different things. According to Tiele this is called theocratic religion, and originated among the Semitic races. The representative religion of the former is Buddhism, while Christianity is the highest development of the latter.

It is quite natural that mechanism or causality grew in the former thought and teleologism or finality comes from the latter. The characteristic of the former religion is tolerance and of the latter intolerance. Von Hartmann gave a suggestion concerning the future religion in his " *Religionsphilosophie.*" According to it the religion which is worthy of the future has to unite these two different tendencies in harmony. But we cannot find the possibility of the unity in the Bible nor in the ordinal Buddhist Scriptures. In other words, there are no foundations on which to unite them in these Sacred Books. In the Bible there is the chapter of " St. John " which accepted abundant pantheistic thought, under the influence of Scholastic philosophy, in order to fill up the original weak point of the Bible. But there is no foundation for uniting them in the whole Bible. Hinayana Buddhism is known as atheism in that it denies the Divine One and only aims at Nirvana. On the other hand, there are pantheism and monotheism in Mahayana Buddhism, for instance, the Shingon Sect, the Zen Sect, the Tendai Sect, etc., belong to pantheism, and the Shin Sect or Jodo Sect belongs to monotheism ; but they also have no foundations on which to unite these opposite tendencies.

Nichirenism is the answer to this problem. First of all, in the Hokekyo, we have the doctrine of " Six Ors " which throws a light on this problem. According to this thought, the Primeval or Fundamental Buddha, whose deep sense of His existence is explained in Chapter XVI in the Scripture, as we have mentioned already, is unique and sole God in the Universe, and all the beings and all the divines or sages and wise men are nothing but His distributive bodies. It says :

" . . . or I explained about my own appearance, or about others' ; or appeared myself, or under the mask of others ; or showed my own action, or others' " (Yamakawa, pp. 459–60 ; cf. Kern, p. 301).

Moreover, it is stated in other lines :

" All young converted men ! Whenever people came and saw me, I considered and observed their different degrees of faculty of faith and so forth, and

I preached the Law under the different names (of Buddhas, gods, sages or wise men, etc.) and the strength of succeeding generations in various places ; and again I revealed my lives and proclaimed that I shall be in Nirvana before long ; and delivered mysterious laws with various pious impositions and allowed beings to feel ecstasy " (Yamakawa, pp. 458–9 ; Kern, p. 300).

Therefore, Nichiren says :

" The Buddha of the 'Duration of the Life of the Tathagata' reveals Himself even in the lives of Grasses (Herbs) and Trees " (Works, p. 1293).

It is evident that in these lines Nichiren's One Buddha Centric Pantheism, as Yamakawa expresses it, is firmly established. And then the following view is possible, that Confucius or Christ or Mohammed or any sages are nothing but one of the distributive bodies of this One and Only Buddha. Nichiren recognized the One Buddha as the sole and highest existence, who revealed Himself as Eternal Buddha in Chapter XVI of the Hokekyo, but at the same time he acknowledged the divine nature as intrinsically inherent in all beings, according to the principle of Mutual Participation of the ten worlds. He holds with monotheism in the former sense and holds with pantheism in the latter sense. But as he says in his letter to a lady, *Nichinyo* (Works, p. 721), he took up the position of One Buddha Centric Pantheism as his ultimate decision. We can see here one of the reasons for determining what the condition of the future religion will be.

Buddhism and Christianity belong to the absolute religion which is acknowledged as the highest development of all religions. Buddhism is called absolute subjective religion and Christianity, absolute objective religion. But it is not so easy to thoroughly unite subjectivism and objectivism in one religion. Religions, in all probability, are one-sided on this point. As I have mentioned before, deistic thought or objective absolutism is prone to modify its main portion to subjective absolutism in order to bring itself into firm existence. For instance, Christianity adopted Greek philosophy, which implies much theanthropic thought, in the effort to remedy its original defect. But, at the same time, the subjective absolutism is liable to fall into atheism after running to excess. The motto in the Zen Sect that states " This mind is Buddha," shows an extreme absolutism, which however causes self-overestimation and denies the pure religious sentiment of absolute dependence on God. Let us take one more example, the Nenbuts Sect (Jodo and Shin Sects) is a typical objective absolutism like Christianity, therefore there is a consistent unity with regard to the religious object and consequently it has a strong religious force, nevertheless there is no possibility of uniting the subjectivism in its system. But it seems that a possible solution of this point is given in Nichiren's doctrine of the Supreme Being :

" There are three in Father : that is, the Myohorengekyo, the Buddha Shakamuni and Nichiren, myself."

This is a paragraph of his " *Ongikuden*," which is a report of his lectures on the Hokekyo in his later days in *Minobu*, and we find in it a similar conception to the theory of the Christian Trinity. The conception of *Myohorengekyo* is the absolute object of our religious faith, but, at the same time, if a man be enlightened and can identify the principle of personality with that of the absolute law in the same breath, then this subject could be harmonized with the object. In other words, it does not mean that we, as we are, are not Buddha Himself, but if we cultivate our Buddha nature and adore the Sacred Title with the most sincere attitude, we can then realize the true innate value of ourselves. Therefore, Nichiren's instruction is given below :

" If you are at One in Faith with me, Nichiren, you are one of the saints-out-of-the-Earth ; and such being your fate, how can you doubt your being the disciple of the Buddha Shakamuni from the earliest ages onward ? Buddha declares : From eternity have I been instructing all these beings (Yamakawa, p. 445 ; Kern, p. 293). No distinction should be made between men and women among those who would propagate the Perfect Truth of the Hokekyo in the days of the Latter Law. To utter the Sacred Title is the privilege of the saints-out-of-the-Earth " (Works, p. 686).

Thus, the religious subject and object can be one and the same by intermediation of " Adoration to the Perfect Truth of the Hokekyo " according to the principle of the Mutual Participation. This thought is worthy of suggestion for the problem of unity of religious subject and object.

Moreover, we can see in this doctrine the relation

between the ideal world and the actual one. It is absolutely useless to seek the ideal world under the name of paradise after completing this life. Of course, we believe in an after-life as well as a past life in a religious sense. But we cannot demonstrate the past nor the after-life, therefore the after-life is possible only as a religious postulation. In short, we must apprehend the meaning of past and future in the very present, hence the present centric consistentism through the three lives, viz. the past, present and future. In respect thereof we shall have a full explanation and idea of Nichiren by our understanding of the doctrine of the Holy See.

Now, let us not neglect another important thought on the Supreme Being. Nichiren wrote down in the Centre of the Supreme Being as follows:

ADORATION TO THE PERFECT MYSTERIOUS LAW ^{SUNGODDESS}_{HACHIMAN} NICHIREN

This, no doubt, indicates a most important thought of Nichiren; it was suggested to him by the doctrine of the *Ten Mysterious Laws of the Honmon* in the Hokekyo. The so-called *Three Radical Mysterious Laws* among the ten are applied in the centre of the Supreme Being.

The Three Radical Mysterious Laws are as under:

1. Mysterious Law of Original Effect.
2. Mysterious Law of Original Cause.
3. Mysterious Law of Original Land.

All of them, originally, were the doctrine concerning the Primeval Buddha. Let us interpret this as far as may be necessary. The Primeval Buddha

who had attained Buddhahood from all eternity, in
other words, the Buddha who revealed Himself as
the eternal saviour in Chapter XVI of the Hokekyo,
reveals Himself in at least the three aspects. First of
all, He reveals Himself as the Perfect Buddha who
is the highest effect of cultivation. That is the
Mysterious Law of Original Effect. It runs in the
Hokekyo as under :

" Listen then, young men of good family. The
force of a strong resolve which I assumed is such,
young men of good family, that this world, including
gods, men, and demons, acknowledges : Now has the
Lord Shakamuni, after going out from the home of
the Shakas, arrived at supreme, perfect enlightenment,
on the summit of the terrace of enlightenment at the
town of Gaya. But, young men of good family, the
truth is that many hundred thousand myriads of
Kotis of Æons ago I have arrived at supreme, perfect
enlightenment. By way of example, young men of
good family, let there be the atoms of earth of fifty
hundred thousand myriads of Kotis of worlds ; let
there exist some man who takes one of those atoms of
dust and then goes in an eastern direction fifty hundred
thousand myriads of Kotis of worlds further on, there
to deposit that atom of dust ; let in this manner the
man carry away from those worlds the whole mass of
earth, and in the same manner, and by the same
act as supposed, deposit all those atoms in an eastern
direction. Now, would you think, young men of
good family, that any one should be able to imagine,
weigh, count, or determine (the number of) those
worlds ? . . . I announce to you, young men of good

family, I declare to you : However numerous be those worlds where that man deposits those atoms of dust and where he does not, there are not, young men of good family, in those hundred thousands of myriads of Kotis of worlds so many dust atoms as there are hundred thousands of myriads of Kotis of Æons since I have arrived at supreme, perfect enlightenment. From the moment, young men of good family, when I began preaching the law to creatures in this Saha-world and in hundred thousands of myriads of Kotis of other worlds " (Kern, pp. 298–300 ; Yamakawa, pp. 455–8).

Secondly, even the Buddha cannot be Buddha without having any cause to be Buddha. Therefore He says :

" Once I had practised the Bodohisattova-course and accomplished the life which is still everlasting, nay, it is multiplied by the *above numbers* " (i.e. 500,000 myriads of Kotis). (Yamakawa, p. 461 ; cp. Kern, p. 303).

The mysterious Law of Original Cause is shown as above. But if such things only are done in heaven then there are nothing but matters-in-heaven. Buddha's contention, however, is quite different from such an imaginary tale ; he, obviously, mentioned such a practice on the earth. Consequently the next problem is the one concerning the background wherein such mysterious things have been actually done. Buddha says :

" From the moment . . . when I began preaching the law to creatures in this *Saha-world*."

Or further :

" And when creatures behold this world and imagine that it is burning, even then my Buddhafield is teeming with gods and men. They dispose of manifold amusements, Kotis of pleasure gardens, palaces, and aerial cars ; (this field) is embellished by hills of gems and by trees abounding with blossoms and fruits. And aloft gods are striking musical instruments and pouring a rain of Mandaras with which they are covering me and the disciples and other sages who are striving after enlightenment. So is my field here, everlastingly ; but others fancy that it is burning ; in their view this world is most terrific, wretched, replete with numbers of woes " (Kern, p. 308 ; Yamakawa, p. 471).

This is the Mysterious Law of Land.

If there be such individuals who practise the Buddha's Way and there are Buddhas, then the country or the world which consists of the above beings must be the ideal world. The Sole Buddha, according to the Hokekyo, reveals Himself in these three aspects, but the three are one. Nichiren founded the system which I mentioned above, from this point of view.

" Namu-Myohorengekyo," " Adoration to the Perfect Truth of the Lotus," means the first " Mysterious Law of Original Effect," " Sungoddess and Hachiman " is the " Mysterious Law of the Original Land " and " Nichiren " means the " Mysterious Law of Original Cause."

Of course, Myohorengekyo is the content of the Buddha Shakamuni's personality, that is to say, it is another name of the Buddha. Therefore, it is quite natural to mention it as the Mysterious Law of Original Effect, namely He manifested the highest effect of attainment of our personality through sincere cultivation.

Nichiren is, of course, in this case, the prophesied person as the executor or performer of the Hokekyo in the age of the Latter Law. There is no doubt that he performed all his duties precisely according to the indication and prophecy of the Hokekyo : that is, he exemplified how to live in order to attain Buddhahood. But the Sungoddess is the Imperial ancestor of Japan, and the God of Hachiman is also a Japanese national God. Herein some people might imagine a narrow-minded notion of nationality, whereas it is, in fact, the most important problem in Nichirenism as the universal religion, and will be fully discussed in Chapter V (Works, pp. 722, 94, 707, 240, 661–6, etc.).

4. THE HOLY ALTAR (HONMON KAIDAN)

The Problem of the Synthetic Creation

The third important thought in Nichirenism is the Holy Altar (or the Holy See). Nichiren founded his most concrete idea of his religious practice on this doctrine. As I have stated above, the Sacred Title was mentioned for the instruction of individuals, the Supreme Being was for the world or universe, and, from this point of view, this Holy Altar is the key to the enlightenment of the country.

Moreover, this Holy Altar, in a sense, is the connection between the Sacred Title and the Supreme Being ; namely the Holy Altar shows the concrete method of entering the Supreme Being, and how to adore the Sacred Title, the essential law of Buddhism. As we shall see later on, the doctrine of the Sacred Title appeared in the early days of Nichiren's activity, and that of the Supreme Being was developed in Sado during his last exile, by which the prophecy of the Hokekyo about him was fully realized. The doctrine of the Holy Altar was proclaimed in the days of his retirement in the recesses of *Minobu*, and is, in fact, the very centre of his religious movement, and upon it his vast system of religion mainly depends. We must therefore examine this thought comparatively and circumstantially.

Let us bear in mind the general idea of the Buddhist Holy Altar prior to Nichiren's statement. The Commandment or precept in Buddhism was valued by all Buddhists, and it was put forward as the sole practical method to attain Buddhahood. Two definitions are given concerning the commandment in Buddhism. The one is " To prevent misdeeds and wickedness " and the other is " To prevent wickedness and do good." In this sense, Hinayana Buddhists have the Five or the Eight or the Ten, or the Two Hundred and Fifty, or the Five Hundred commandments, according to their different conditions ; and Mahayana Buddhists also have the Tenfold or the Forty-eight commandments. There are besides, special commandments in the Hokekyo, the one is the Shakumon Centric Commandment and the other is the Honmon Centric one. Laymen, monks, nuns and all sorts of human beings are entreated to keep these commandments. However, all these commandments can be comprised in two parts according to their essential meanings. Formal commandment is the one and Idealistic commandment is the other. For instance, all Hinayanistic Commandments and those of the general Mahayanism belong to the formal commandments, while the commandment of the Hokekyo belongs to the idealistic one. From the point of view of the former, all the rules must be kept by people formally, while the deep idea of commandment is associated with the latter. We can say nothing about the history of the development of the commandments here, nevertheless, it is evident that the vicissitudes of the Buddhist commandment can fairly be compared with the rise and fall of the doctrine which I have previously stated.

The Great Master Dengyo, with reference to this, adopted the Shakumon centric idealistic commandment, while he rejected the Hinayanistic ones and those of the general Mahayanism. Dengyo, however, held, with the Shakumon centric commandment, the former fourteen chapters of the Hokekyo ; therefore, he could not go further with the Honmon. Consequently, he adopted the Tenfold Prohibitive Commandments of the *Bonmokyo* (Skt. Brahma Djāla Sūtra), holding at the same time with the Shakumon centric idealistic commandment.

Nichiren, on the contrary, adopted only the Honmon centric one and strictly prohibited any other kinds ; because he saw the reason from the fact and the proof of the Scriptures that there is no authority maintained concerning the formal commandment in the days of the Latter Law. It would be too ineffectual to stipulate that a man should be such and such only by formal rules in this world of five turbidities or impurities.

We must attach more essential significance to commandment by refraining from such external rules; in other words, it is much more important to give signification of life in the depths of people's minds than to give the ordinal arrangement of actions and appearances. Of course, there is no doubt that these old-fashioned commandments were very effective at one time in early ages, but are too formal and too powerless to adapt to the age of the Latter Law. The age and people must have more internal authority, namely the commandment must be such as to give fundamental rules in the internal personality, with the most simple and authoritative dignity. Nichiren, therefore, rejected the Hinayanistic and general Mahayanistic commandments in consideration of their powerlessness, and, it may be added, with the authority of many Buddhist Scriptures on this point. He says :

" Now, the commandments are the Hinayanistic Two Hundred and Fifty rules. . . . With reference to the first commandment, namely ' Thou shalt kill no living being,' in all the Scriptures except the Hokekyo, it is said that the Buddha kept this law. But the Buddha, who is revealed in these Scriptures with pious imposition, starts by killing, so to speak, from the point of view of the Hokekyo. Why? Because, although it seemed that the Buddha in these Scriptures kept the law in His daily affairs, yet He did not keep the True Commandment of ' Kill no living being ' : because He killed the possibility of

Attainment of Buddhahood of all other beings except Buddhas Themselves, so that the beings were not allowed to attain Buddhahood. Thus, the leader, the Buddha, is not yet released from the sin of Killing, how much less the disciples" (Works, pp. 365–6).

Therefore, Nichiren gives significance to one's free will, which means in a sense an imperative category. This is a different point from that of the ordinal commandment which governs several of our acts superficially. He united the teachings and commandments which are explained together in the *Nehangyo*, from the point of view of the doctrine of the Hokekyo. Although a man makes himself a perfect Buddhist, if it is limited to a mere individual personality and has no positive effect in protecting and spreading the Buddhist Law, then all exertions are in vain. However much one may be faithful to the mere individual formal commandment, it is of no use unless one awakes to the signification of one's existence. Thus Nichiren thought. According to him, the signification of one's existence can be filled up with ardent vows for the protection and enlargement of the Law.

Nichiren saw the Mysterious Law of the Hokekyo in the very mysterious power whereby people do righteousness and goodness, even though they be bad and evil. If the Attainment of Buddhahood were only granted to those possessing a perfect personality from every point of view, then the Attainment of Buddhahood would be an imagination. Even a man with defects in his character, if he awakes to the signification of life, that is to the protection and enlargement of the perfect Law, and if he acts according to this ideal, then his act is equivalent to that of the Buddha-course, notwithstanding that his defects are not yet eliminated. Of course, according to Nichiren's view, the moral cultivation of individuals is doubtless important, but belongs rather to common sense, and is therefore treated in the doctrine of the "Four Instructive Methods" (*Shi-shits-dan*). One of the paragraphs in the Hokekyo which was very often cited by Nichiren as the demonstration of this thought is to the following effect :

" Not only I myself shall be pleased, but the Lords of the world in general, if one would keep for a moment this Sutra so difficult to keep. Such a one shall ever be praised by all the Lords of the world. Such is courageousness, such is assiduous advance (Skt. Vīrya; Japanese, Shōjin). I call such a man the true *practitioner of Buddhism* (Skt. Dhūta; Japanese, Zuda) and the true keeper of the commandment " (Yamakawa, pp. 363–4 ; Kern, p. 242. This translation is partly Kern's and partly mine.)

To transfer the ideal of the Hokekyo to man's daily life is equivalent to keeping the commandment. This is the commandment of the Hokekyo. In other words, the *namu* or to devote oneself to the propagation of the Law of the Scripture is equivalent to " Keeping the Commandment." From this point of view Nichiren saw two aspects of the commandment of the Hokekyo, that is self-devotion to the essential law of the Hokekyo and its realization and extension to the whole world. In order to spread this law over the world, some attacks must be made on all kinds of evil : nay, it is absolutely necessary to eradicate the evil. This was suggested to him by the *Nehangyo* (Skt. Mahāparinirvāṇa-sūtra or the Scripture of Buddha's Great Decease) and the Hokekyo. On the one hand, he proclaimed that " To keep the Sacred Title is the commandment." He says :

" The five characters of Myohorengekyo, the essence of the Honmon of the Hokekyo, are stated as the assemblage of all virtues of all the Buddhas in the past, in the present, and even in the future. Why should not the five characters contain all virtues and effects of all the commandments " (Works, p. 324).

We must also not neglect the following results which are cited by Nichiren (from the Nehangyo) very often as being one of his thoughts about the commandment. It says :

" However virtuous a priest may be, if he neglects to eject transgressors, to make them repent or renounce their sins, hearken ! he is wicked and hostile to Buddhist Law. If he casts them out to make them be repentant and amend their negligence, he is worthy to be my disciple and truly virtuous."

Thus the idea of the Hokekyo does not admit of a mere self-complacency in faith, but it demands absolute reconstruction and instructing one's environments. Therefore, the definition of faith is much different from the ordinal ones in other religions. The significant purport of a Nichirenian's faith must be a combination of both, which is self-devotion and social reconstruction, therefore he says :

" How grievous it is that we were born in such a

country wherein the right law is disparaged and we suffer great torment ! How shall we deal with the unbelief in our homes and in our country, even though some people observe the faith of the Law whereby they are relieved of the sin of individual disparagement. If you desire to relieve your home of unbelief, tell the truth of the Scripture to your parents, brothers and sisters. What would happen would be detestation or belief. If you desire the State to be the righteous one you must remonstrate with the King or the government on its disparagement of the righteous law, at the risk of capital punishment or banishment. . . . From all eternity, all failures of people to attain Buddhahood were rooted in silence about this, out of fear of such things '' (Works, p. 651).

The conception of the commandment, therefore, is not merely negative virtue of individuals, but undoubtedly a strong vow for the realization of a universal or humanistic ideal paradise in this world.

According to Nichiren, the heavenly paradise has not an allegorical existence, but is the highest aim of living beings in the living world, in other words, it must be actually built on the earth. For such a fundamental humanistic aim we must all strive. The true commandment has not its being apart from the vow. If one fully comprehends his thought, and will strive for it, then the signification of one's life will be realized. This thought is the most important idea of Nichiren's religion, and, in fact, the peculiarity of Nichirenism consists therein. For him, to protect and extend the righteousness over the world, through the country and to everybody is the true task of life.

Consequently, he tested what would be the most convenient way of realizing such an ideal in the world, and he found the country for it.

The country or the state, of course, is the secondary production of human life because of the order of its origination, but as a matter of fact, with regard to our present civilized world, individual beings are preceded by the country. With regard to the method of salvation, the country must be classed as the unit. All existing methods therein are in all probability mere individual standards ; on the contrary it is the country or the state standard as regards Nichirenism. Of course, as we have already mentioned, the country or the state is without doubt the highest civilization, and the world is divided into various countries, and all the individuals, too, are divided into several nations. Consequently, the world in accordance with observation, from a point of view of the methodical system, cannot exist apart from the countries. The individual cannot live without the country, or I should say the individual who does not belong to any country, if such there be, could not demand or be entitled to civilization.

In the religious sense, the unification of the world or the salvation of the world is impossible unless the religion and the country assimilate. Nichiren, therefore, determined the country as the unit of salvation of the world as far as method is concerned. He says :

" Hearken ! the country will prosper with the moral law, and the law is precious when practised by man. If the country be ruined and human beings collapse, who would worship the Buddha, who would believe the law ?   First of all, therefore, pray for the security of the country and afterwards establish the Buddhist Law " (Works, p. 13).

This is a paragraph in his important essay, " *Rissho Ankoku-ron* " or " An Essay on the Establishment of Righteousness and Security of the Country."   He discoursed on the relation between the country and religion in this essay and sent it to the Hojos Government at an early date as an intimation of his religious movement ;   but this thought fully developed by degrees and eventually the doctrine of the Holy Altar was founded.   There is no doubt that Nichiren thus thought of the country as the most concrete basis on which to propagate religion.

The intention of realizing a religious paradise by the purification of each individual might be compared with a person vainly calculating to disprove the decimal system.   It would be like fresh and savoury meat being placed on an unclean dish, thereby destroying the flavour of the good meat.   However righteous each individual might be, if his environment, which is the country, be greedy, his Attainment of Buddhahood would be, to put it briefly, incomplete.

Therefore, as remarked by me in the introduction, the standard of the religious cultivation must be determined by the congregational body, the representative of which is the country.   The country contains various things, viz. the subject and object of sovereignty, diverse societies, education, law, military force and economical power, etc. etc.   These things have a concrete influence on the nation, not even a single one of them can be neglected.   Consequently, the religion of the future shall have all these things as objects of salvation. Religion is intended to redeem living beings and their environment. Therefore, religion must purify the whole concrete life of man in order to religionize all individuals and the world. If religion does not in any sense concern material life, but merely spiritual life, then is religious influence almost in vain. A belief which purposely eliminates material affairs from the religious field is not only a misunderstanding of the essential meaning of religion, but is a very wrong view of human life. The true religious Empire can be established in the material world which is purified with spiritual signification. Nichiren's doctrine of the Holy Altar is, indeed, an enlightenment of religion with material purification. To unite the spiritual force and the material may have been discussed in the past, but it still remains unsolved. The lopsidedness of spiritualism in the field of religion has caused the present weakness and inefficiency of all religion in spite of preachings. Enlightenment and guidance to the material life is an absolute necessity if man does not live spiritually only. The country, in this sense, is the representative material organization, so to speak. In fact, human life is saved, is protected, and is watched over by the country. The individuals form the country and society, despite individuals being forced to control their concrete lives. Of course the individual has the supernational will, but he is forced to obey the national laws. It is evident that international society is now becoming of much greater significance than the country in human life; international society is wider and higher than the country, or at least the racial combination is stronger than society. Of course, according to modern interpretation, Nichiren's thought of the country naturally implies two aspects which are the country and society. At any rate, for him, such a combined body of human lives was thought most important for the religious salvation of the world. The country is not the ultimate aim of the human ideal, it must be the universal ideal society, consequently, the country must be such as to have ultimately a purposive unity in joint existence or co-operative aim. While the existing countries have no fixed idea on this point, correspondingly so many countries are the greedy enemies of one another. Therefore, to realize the ultimate human ideal world we must, to begin with, reconstruct the country so that it may exist hand in hand with righteousness.

According to Nichiren, in the degenerate days of the Latter Law, there is no Buddhist commandment outside of our vow for the reconstruction of the country and the realization of the Heavenly Paradise in the world. Even the so-called virtuous sage, if he does not embrace this great and strong vow, in other words only enjoys virtue individually, such a sage is pretty useless.

Although a man be imperfect, let him carry out Buddha's task with the strong vow for the realization of Buddha's Kingdom, with preaching or with economical power or with knowledge of sciences and with all sorts of such things. We can find the true significance of religion, of commandment, of human life therein.

The protection of moral law is the sole task of human life, and this is the greatest invention and discovery of our lives. When one digresses from and acts against the moral principle, one is no longer worthy of being a human being, thus Nichiren thought. Consequently, weapons, army, education, commerce or the life, everything must be for the sake of true human life, which means the practice and the protection of moral laws. Buddha says in the Nehangyo :

" In spite of a man accepting and keeping the Five Commandments, he cannot be called a man of the true Mahayana Buddhism. One who protects the right law is the man of the true Mahayana Buddhism, even though he does not keep the Five Commandments. The man who protects the right law shall be armed. Him do I call the true practitioner of the Buddhist Commandments though he is armed."

This thought is also apparent in the Hokekyo. It says in Chapter XIV :

" It is a case, *Mangusri* (Japanese, *Monju* or *Monjushiri*), similar to that of a *King* (Tenrinjo-o; Skt. Chakravarti-raja), a ruler of armies, who by force has conquered his own Kingdom, whereupon other Kings, his adversaries, wage war against him. That ruler of armies has soldiers of various descriptions to fight with various enemies. As the King sees those soldiers fighting, he is delighted with their gallantry, enraptured, and in his delight and rapture he makes to his soldiers several donations, such as villages and village ground, towns and grounds of a town ; garments and head-gear ; hand-ornaments, necklaces, gold threads, ear-rings, strings of pearls, bullion, gold, gems, pearls, lapis lazuli, conch-shells, stones (?), corals ; he, moreover, gives elephants, horses, cars, foot soldiers, male and female slaves, vehicles and litters " (Kern, p. 274 ; Yamakawa, p. 415).

Therefore, Nichiren proclaims :

" Know ye, that when these Bodohisattovas act in accordance with the positive instruction, they will appear as wise kings and attack foolish kings in order to instruct them ; when they will act negatively then will they appear as priests and propagate and keep the right law " (Works, p. 103).

In that relation did Nichiren acknowledge military force, he accordingly wrote an instruction to one of his great supporters, Shijo Kingo, who was a typical Japanese warrior :

" Prefer the art of war to any other art, even any branch connected therewith shall be rooted in the Law of the Hokekyo " (Works, p. 907).

Of course in this connection it is not his intention to interfere with anything relating to the substance itself, but it is mentioned for the fundamental enlightenment of all existence. In this relation Buddha makes the following suggestions :

" All the pluralistic laws which are preached in several instances, do not contradict nor contravene Suchness by their signification. Even the moral books in the world or political words or industry or the like may be explained to the people, they shall all comply with the right law " (Yamakawa, pp. 539–40 ; there are no equivalent lines in Kern).

Hereupon Nichiren emancipated the ordinal conception of religion into the broadest sense, which is the synthetic creation. *The moral books* in the above quotation, imply philosophy, ethics, literature or the like ; *political words* mean legislation, the judicature and administration, and *industry* means agriculture, commerce and the manufacturing industry, etc. Nichiren gave this instruction to his disciples :

" The priests among my disciples shall be the Masters to the Emperors or the ex-Emperors, and the laymen shall take seats in the Ministry ; and thus in the future, all the nations in the world shall adore this law " (Works, p. 583).

He goes on to say :

" In brief, my religion is the law of the political path " (Works, p. 391).

Therefore, for Nichiren, the professional practice of religion is not only the method, but verily also the justification and purification of our daily lives at every turn. Keeping this in mind, read the following instruction of Nichiren to Shijo Kingo.

" Consider your daily works in your Lord's service as being the practice of the Hokekyo " (Works, p. 893).

Thus, he established the religious method of the synthetic creation, and he decided that the country should be the unit of the worldly salvation. Summing up the salient points, according to Nichiren, if religion really wants to redeem the world, it must religionize the country. Religion as it is cannot religionize the country ; it is not worthy of the future religion. He thought that the state is the unit of the world, and that the individual could never be the unit of the world. In other words, it is useless to uphold the fallacy that if religion instructs individuals one by one, the world, will, naturally, sooner or later, become religionized. On the contrary, let us suppose that the state has the conviction of true morality, and of politics, education and diplomacy, or that everything has been done morally ; then the individual who belongs to the state is, as it were, a snake in a narrow and straight bamboo-tube. It may seem like bondage, nevertheless such a right bondage must be welcomed. Is the so-called free will surely free ? Man cannot live without being to a certain extent in bondage, though one may be proud to live and decide everything by one's own free will, for free will, too, is a sort of bondage. Year after year, as readers know, theories and books on ethics are ever increasing, year by year, the numberless doctrines and scriptures of religion are appearing, from year to year, churches, temples and schools are multiplying, but inversely the world and mankind are deteriorating, and criminal statistics are increasing in number as years roll on. Are these not notable phenomena ? Hence the country that is moral must take up as her mission the task of the guardianship and espousal of truth, morality and righteousness with all her accumulated power. However religionized a man may be, if the country is not made just, then even the man of righteousness is liable to be obliged to commit a crime in an emergency for the sake of a nation's covetous disposition. The existing countries of the world are committing monstrous self-contradictions of morality. There is no reason at all for a country to be allowed to do wrong under the pretence of so-called " For the sake of the country," while the country prohibits all lawlessness and iniquity of the individuals therein. So, to start with, such a fallacy must be eliminated. Nichiren, therefore, examined the essence of the various countries and he decided upon Japan as being the typical moral country. According to Nichiren, Japan is distinctly the typical country based on strict morality, consequently the mission of Japan consists in setting an example of the moral country to the world (see *infra*, Chapter V). Therefore, he says :

" The first and great Supreme Being shall be established in this country " (Works, p. 104).

Of course, he does not proclaim the monistic theory of the country, but he found an ideal country which is a standard for the pluralistic countries of the world. Nichiren believed the fated destination between the Hokekyo and Japan and between Japan and Nichiren himself as Honge Jogyo. He says :

" The Great Master Myoraku says (in his Commentary) : The children benefit the world by propagating the law of the Father : *Children* means here the Saints-out-of-the-earth ; *Father* means the Buddha Shakamuni ; *World* signifies Japan ; *Benefit* the Attainment of Buddhahood ; *Law* the adoration of the Myohorengekyo. It is now the same as ever it was, *Father* is Nichiren ; *Children* are my, Nichiren's, disciples and adherents ; *World* is Japan ; *Benefit* means accepting and keeping this law and thereby accomplishing the Attainment of Buddhahood ; and *Law* is the Sacred Title bequeathed to us by Honge Jogyo " (" Ongikuden ").

But we must be conscious that the " *World is Japan.*" This is not to be taken literally in this translation nor in the original.

Anesaki gives the following explanation :

" In this latter sense, Japan meant for him the whole world " (Anesaki, " Nichiren, the Buddhist Prophet." Harvard University Press, p. 98).

But this appears to be incorrect because the character of " *the World* " does not mean here the world in the usual sense, but it means " the World-Benefit," namely one of the Four Siddhanta, the Four Instructive Methods (*Shi-shits-dan*). In other words, this is a special technical term, the full name is " The Completion of the world with the benefit of delight " (*Sekai Shits-dan Kangi no Yaku*). Hence, " *the World is Japan* " means " Japan has the mission to propagate the law of the Hokekyo and thereby redeem the world."

As we have seen above, Nichiren beheld the signification of the relation between the Hokekyo and Nichiren himself through the fact of the wonderful combination of Japan. According to him the world must be united as brethren, namely as a moral world, and in the future the Holy Altar of the Hokekyo, especially of the Honmon centric commandment, shall be established in Japan. He says in one of his significant essays, " On the Three Great Secret Laws " (*San dai Hihō Shō*).

" At a certain future time, when the state law will unite with the Buddhist law and the Buddhist law harmonizes with the state law, and both sovereign and subjects will keep sincerely the Three Secret Laws, then will be realized such a golden age in the degeneration of the Latter Law, as it was in olden times under the rule of King *Utoku*. Thus the Holy Altar will be established with Imperial Sanction or the like at a place like the excellent paradise of Vulture Peak. We must only prepare and await the advent of the time. There is no other law or commandment which is practicable, only this one. This Holy Altar is not only the sanctuary for all nations of three countries (India, China and Japan) and the whole world, but even the great deities, Brahma and Indra, have to descend in order to initiate into the perfect truth of the Hokekyo " (Works, pp. 240–41).

Once Ibsen proclaimed " The Third Empire." Nichiren had systematized and proclaimed it nearly seven hundred years ago. Thus, he established the Three Great Secret Laws and left them to deal with the future world. Nichiren's religion is, in fact, the principle of synthetic creation. Therefore in Nichirenism everything can be brought into harmonization. It is evident that he proclaims the necessity of subjecting all countries to one moral law, approving, of course, the pluralistic existence of all countries. But it is totally different from the Utopian's fancy, because of his positive adoption of all material forces.

Therefore the commandment of his religion is recognized by the act of keeping and practising the

Hokekyo for his own sake and at the same time for the sake of human kind. Consequently, the vow and its practice are the essential elements in his religion. In order to keep the law bodily means that in daily life we must be determined to do anything. Rich men shall protect the law by means of their wealth and learned men shall extend the law by means of their knowledge and wisdom, etc. All the accumulated power of human civilization must make it a duty to help to realize the law on the earth. In an emergency, we shall be martyrs to the law. In short, we must keep the law for dear life and then the sincerity and signification of life will be realized. Such being the case with individuals, the country, too, must be established on righteousness. The country is, indeed, an organ for the realization of the moral law of security with all her accumulated powers. When the country attains to such conviction that it becomes the highest organ for the protection of righteousness, and that it can sacrifice itself whenever it is obliged to do so for the sake of the law, then the ideal world will be realized before our very eyes. The Holy Altar is mentioned for this purpose.

To realize this ideal we are expected to have absolute faith even at the risk of our lives. Although persecution, innumerable difficulties and troubles might be our lot we could go through fire and water if our faith were strong and true. Nichiren exclaims with firm conviction :

" It appears to be the age when the five characters of Myohorengekyo, which is the essence of the Scripture, which is the principal object in view of all

I

the Buddhas, shall be propagated over the world, which is the beginning of the Latter Law. At this time, I, Nichiren, have taken upon myself the task of pioneering, although even those great men, Kasho and Anan, etc., Memyo and Ryuju, etc., and Nangaku, Tendai, Myoraku and Dengyo had not propagated this law for over 2220 years since Buddha's Death : My young men and women, ye shall come in quick succession, and excel, in the propagation of this law, those sages Kasho and Anan and likewise those great men Tendai and Dengyo. If you stand in fear of threats by *the King or the like* (the Hojos and the official authorities) of so small an island, how would you fare if you confronted *Enma's* Throne of Judgment " (Works, p. 393).

Nichirenism, as already stated, taught us the most sincere vow for dear life in order to render life significant and truly happy, and now the modern Nichirenism teaches us how to realize such an ideal in the world. Thus a Nichirenian's idealism is not a mere spiritualism, but a concrete motion with material forces, it is possible therefore for direct action to follow in an emergency.

Imaginative gods, fanciful views of reality, superstitions, and egoistic faith are, all of them, denied in Nichirenism. These Three Great Secret Laws are the Key to the future civilization. Recent civilization has brought about the freedom of the masses and equality by depriving the nobility of their freedom. Although people may call their own action righteousness, it is, indeed, merely freedom and equality of the commons just as it was arbitrariness in the case of the nobility.

In Nichiren's thought such one-sided righteousness is denied absolutely.

Nichiren expected to establish his ideal country, heaven on earth, by the incessant efforts of all his followers in the future. But the world will fall into evil ways, nay into folly with its struggles; for instance, capitalism against labour, socialism against aristocratism, individualism against nationalism, diabolism against humanism, etc., while religion or ethics is constantly somniloquising. Finally, the world might fall into extreme confusion just like modern Russia. Should it happen thus, all human beings and all countries would awaken and heed Nichiren's warning, so thought Nichiren. He speaks the following words :

" At a future time, a war more stupendous than any before will be waged, when it comes all beings under the light of the Sun and Moon will pray for mercy to all manner of Buddhas and Bodohisattovas out of fear of the ruin of their countries or lives : If in spite of that they do not receive divine favour, then, for the first time, innumerable priests and all the great kings will believe the hated priestling (i.e. Nichiren himself), and all people will call upon the Sacred Title, making the sincerest vows and joining hands, just as when the Buddha performed the Ten Mysterious Powers (miracles) in Chapter XXI of the Hokekyo, and all existence without exception in the ten directions, shouted 'Adoration to the Buddha Shakamuni, Adoration to the Buddha Shakamuni and Adoration to the Perfect Truth of the Hokekyo, Adoration to the Perfect Truth of the Hokekyo ' towards this world loudly in the same breath" (Works, p. 111; and see Tanaka: " Nichiren's Doctrine ").

Nichiren's religion was founded with such a future aim, and was not well understood at that time nor even at the present day. But the time is drawing nigh when this religion will be accepted. The Great War, in a sense, may be an omen that Nichiren mentioned when he said the greatest war on record. To the problem between the country and religion, or that of ethics and religion, the Key of possible solution is given here, I think.

Now let us learn about the life Nichiren led and how he came upon these remarkable thoughts and the reason for his special admiration of Japan.

IV

NICHIREN'S LIFE

1. Circumstances

To begin with, let us state the circumstances which happened surrounding Nichiren's birth :

Nichiren was born in 1222. Japan had a most significant time historically just then, alike politically, religiously and socially.

Some seven hundred years had elapsed since Buddhism had been introduced into Japan, and it had been totally Japanesed at that time. There were several sects, several schools, numerous priests and scholars, thousands of temples : it seemed as if they were showing the glorious day of Buddhism. From an historical point of view of Buddhist doctrine, this time was the age of the general Mahayana Buddhism, while the Hinayana Buddhism was decaying. It was the beginning of the Latter Law, and by this time all Buddhist sects had fully developed.

The so-called *Six sects of the old capital* were, of course, in their prime soon after Buddhism was introduced into the country. Instead of them, the mixed sect, the Tendai-Shingon Secret Sect took their place, and soon after the famous battle age of Japanese Buddhism came about. During the Kamakura period of Japanese history, especially as regards religion, the people's religious consciousness and ideas ripened into maturity, and thus many sects were established in succession after the battles between the two clans, the *Minamotos* and *Tairas* (or *Genji* and *Heike*). In particular the Zen and Nenbuts sects, as the new rising religions, were welcomed among the people, while the Shingon Sect was in favour at Court. Further, *Ryōnin, Honen, Eisai* and *Shinran*, etc., founded their own sects.

From about the middle of the Fanciful Law to Nichiren's establishment of his religion, many sects came into existence as abundantly as mushrooms after rain, but no sect has been founded since Nichiren established the Hokekyo centric religion. At any rate, the circumstances of his day thus, in a sense, were at the time of the religious climax, and all the sects asserted themselves as the right Buddhism.

On the other hand, in the political sphere, the real power of politics was transferred to the military clans in inverse ratio to the falling off.

Court-nobles for a long time had indulged in every luxury and lost their actual power by degrees, while the military clans esteemed and fostered real ability more than titles of honour which were but empty titles.

The Minamotos had been holding the real power of politics prior to Nichiren's birth, and they established the central government at Kamakura far from the western Capital Kyoto. The military clan's government was already on a secure foundation, although the Hojos took the place of the Minamotos when he was born. The Hojos stuck to real ability and enforced strict modesty. They thus seized the political power of the country and consequently they were apt to interfere with the Court and Court-nobles. It had the effect of the ex-Emperor *Gotoba* wanting to wage war against the Hojos Government in order to recover political power. As soon as an urgent message was sent to the Hojos Government, *Hojo Yoshitoki, the Shikken* (the highest representative of the Government), sent an army against the Court troops. Unfortunately the Court troops were defeated and the Hojos' army made a raid on the Court's territory. Hereupon Hojo Yoskitoki usurped the Court and expelled three ex-Emperors to far islands remote from each other. Yoshitoki set one of H.I.H. princes on the throne who was in no way concerned with the war.

Such a terrible event, indeed, never before occurred and never must occur again in Japan, where the relation and task between sovereign and subject are strictly distinguished on the understanding and faith of the Japanese National Principles. It was in the third year of *Shokyu*, the 1881st year after the Accession of the Emperor Jimmu, that is to say, 1221st year of the Christian Era. Hence the Shokyu War.

2.   His Birth and Studies

He was born on the 16th of the second month of the fourth year of Shokyu, which is just one year later than the Shokyu War. His father lived on the sea coast of Awa, a province of the eastern part of Japan, as a poor fisherman (Works, pp. 616, 792, 463, 1536, etc.)

His native village faces the Pacific Ocean and is near a quiet hill. He lived with his parents until he was twelve years of age. We are not intimately acquainted with the details of his family because he seldom wrote giving particulars. Of course, there are many traditions about his lineage and his childhood, but they do not affect his true life to any extent. We shall therefore omit them.

As years rolled on, this infant prodigy became distinct from all others, and when he became twelve years of age reason was beginning to bud in his mind. He gave vent to his great doubt concerning the contradictory facts of the country with regard to the most important things. What were they ? According to one of his extant autographical manuscripts, he harboured two serious doubts, the one was about religion and the other about the Shokyu War, with reference to the Japanese National Principles and history. He writes in one of his letters :

" As you know, I studied diligently from my boyhood, and I prayed to the Bodohisattova *Kokuzō* since I was twelve years of age in order that I should be made the wisest man in Japan. But, for certain reasons, I cannot write about it minutely yet " (Works (the Ryogonkaku Edition), Second Series, p. 88 ; the manuscripts in Nichiren's own handwriting are extant. Cf. Works, p. 1543).

Buddha's true teaching must be one, though there exist thousands of different doctrines with pious-imposition ; however, Buddhism in general was contradictory at that time. Nichiren, first of all very much questioned such Buddhism. In the second place, he could not neglect the Shokyu War which had happened one year before his birth. Why was the Sovereign's army beaten by the Hojo's? And why do not people doubt such a topsyturvy, a mere subject like Hojo Yoskitoki daring to expel the three ex-Emperors to islands? Without doubt, Nichiren wanted to solve these marvellous questions, so he made up his mind to go to the Buddhist Monastery to enable him to get at the root of such phenomena. He says :

" The seven sects of Mahayanism sing their own praises as follows : Our Sect is the important essence of the whole Buddhism, etc. . . . People say : We, common people, can be satisfied with any master or priest by believing him. It might be the best way to revere and believe any priest ; but my, Nichiren's, doubt has not been dispelled. Although every individual tries to get ahead of all others, yet the Sovereign must be one ; if two Kings co-exist in one country there cannot be peace ; if there are two masters in one home, then family dissensions will break out. It is not otherwise in Buddhism. Apart from what it is, one Scripture must be the great King of all the Buddhist Scriptures. Nevertheless, the ten Sects and the seven sects, all of them, still discuss the problem and each one individually claims to be the great King of Buddhism, just as in the case of a people being in a state of confusion under seven or ten kings. I was once at sixes and sevens and harboured a doubt on this point to solve the problem " (Works, p. 154).

This is an expression of his doubt regarding Buddhism, and the other, his doubt regarding the

Shokyu War, is to be seen in one of his essays. About the affairs of the war, he writes :

" When I began to study exoterics and esoterics seriously and all the Scriptures which are adopted by all the sects, I studied sometimes from masters, sometimes by myself, and sometimes I made researches ; I thought over and over and at last hit upon a way of settling the doubt which I harboured on the Shokyu War from my very boyhood " (Works, p. 524 ; cf. *ibid.*, pp. 586, 1543, 1096, 1653–4, 357, 1570, 929, etc. Ref., pp. 408, 1098).

Thus his religious awakening occurred voluntarily, so he at last resolved to study the questions in order to solve his great doubts. He left his parents' home behind with their consent in the beginning of summer 1233. He entered the monastery of *Kiyosumi*, which is not far from his parents' home, but kept aloof from earthly affairs. He began to study Buddhism, Brahmanism, Confucianism and Japanese literature, etc., under the Master *Dozen's* direction. He changed his name from *Zen-nichimaro* to *Yakuōmaro*. This Yakuomaro studied with all his might day and night to satisfy his great ambition to become " The wisest man in Japan." When he reached the age of sixteen he entered the priesthood and changed his name to *Rencho*. He read all the books in this monastery, not leaving a single book there unread. He then left Kiyosumi for Kamakura in this year 1238, or very soon after (Works, pp. 354, 586, 421).

Kamakura was then the seat of the Government, and at that time there were many eminent scholars who lived there. He spent several years in Kamakura making deep researches into the Zen Sect and the Nenbuts (or Jodo) Sect. He then left Kamakura for Kiyosumi, where he wrote his maiden essay (Works, p. 1655, " Kaitai-Sokushin-Jōbuts-gi " means An Essay on the Attainment of Buddhahood by the Substance of the Commandment).

Although he pointed out in that book the fallacy of the Jodo Sect from the point of view of the Hokekyo, yet he praised the esoterics of the Shingon Sect above the Hokekyo. Nichiren, nay, Rencho, could no longer feel satisfied with the Buddhist scholars in the provinces. So, he went to the monastery of Hiei near the Capital, Kyoto, where he stayed from 1243 to 1253. The monastery of Hiei was the authoritative centre of Buddhism, and there were three thousand independent monasteries there. He sought knowledge extensively and made deep researches not only into Dengyo's doctrine, but into all the doctrines of all sects, and several other branches of science. He stayed mainly in Hiei, but sometimes he went on journeys to various places where there were authorities in their own way of sciences. It is said that he read all the Buddhist Scriptures four times over during his stay in this mountain. At all events there is no doubt that he accomplished the bulk of what he aimed at during the few years which he spent there.

Through his long and thorough researches he at last arrived at his climax, viz. that the Hokekyo was the sole ultimate adoration for the people. The Great Master Dengyo, the founder of Hiei, was the right master of the Hokekyo, none the less his successors took the wrong way at that time, or I should say, the Great Masters *Jikaku* and *Chisho*, who were

Dengyo's disciples, adopted Shingon-secularism which they mixed with the doctrine of the Hokekyo. They proclaimed that the theories of the Hokekyo and Shingon-mysticism were quite one and the same, but that the latter was superior to the former in a practical sense. Nichiren saw the greatest fallacy therein, and denounced these two masters' views to the public when an academical council was held in Hiei. He says :

" Jikaku and Chisho pretend to be true disciples of the Great Master Dengyo, but in reality they are not true disciples of his. . . . According to this proclamation, Jikaku and Chisho are the traitors of the late master, if ever there were any " (Works, p. 171. Ref., *ibid.*, p. 175).

3. His Proclamation to the Universe

Thus it is clearly evident that at that time the school of Dengyo very much deviated from Dengyo's right view. This fact once disappointed him when he saw the light, but he immediately resolved to resuscitate the right teaching of Dengyo and begin the movement of the Hokekyo. He visited Dengyo's grave on the hill and mourned over his soul, at the loss of his right teaching. Nichiren left Hiei for his native village, where his parents and his old master were still alive awaiting their loving boy and disciple.

Now, he feels it incumbent upon him to say something about his learning, and from the conclusion he had drawn it must be most faithful and strong advice which, though it might sound harsh to the people's ears, must be uttered. It is also written in the Hokekyo, that in consequence of those who will propagate the Law in the beginning of the Latter Law against all the sects and all people, many dreadful persecutions shall threaten him. And Nichiren knew it too clearly ; but he was a man. He fell into mental agony concerning "*to be persecuted*" or "*not to be persecuted.*" He thought and thought night and day, and at last resolved on denouncement, while all the neighbours welcomed him, expecting to hear graceful sermons about the Amita Buddhism.

Nichiren retired for a week to a quiet room in the forest, near the monastery of Kiyosumi. As soon as he had prepared himself there Nichiren left the forest house at dawn and climbed the summit of the hill which commands the vast expanse of the Pacific Ocean.

Motionless he stood looking Eastward ; a loud voice broke forth from his lips, saying, " Namu-Myohorengekyo, Adoration to the Perfect Truth of the Lotus ! " When the golden disc of the sun began to break, it was to heaven and earth that Nichiren's proclamation of his new religion was made, calling the all-illuminating sun to witness. This happened at dawn of the 28th day of April, 1253.

After this proclamation to the universe he got his new name of Nichiren, which means " Sun-Lotus," suggested by the Hokekyo (see Works, pp. 609, 1054, 845). Nichiren began to descend the hill in an extreme ecstasy and came back among the people. At noon of the same day he preached for the first time his unique religion based on the Hokekyo, in a service room facing south. Alas ! quite contrary to the hearers' expectation, Nichiren denounced all the wrong Buddhism in the presence of his parents and friends, his old master and the neighbours. Thereupon their prodigious astonishment turned into persecution. Nichiren was banished for ever from his old master's monastery, while only his parents among all who heard him were believers.

He thought, at this time, of one of the stanzas of " Exertion " in the Hokekyo. It runs :

" One will have to bear frowning looks, repeated disavowal (or concealment), expulsion from the monasteries, many and manifold abuses " (Kern, p. 261 ; Yamakawa, p. 392).

On the first day of his propagation of the Hokekyo, he had already had experience of persecution. He looks back upon the past in later days and he writes :

" Once I received the greatest wisdom from the deity Kokuzo. It may have been that he responded to my supplication, which was : Have mercy upon me and make of me Japan's wisest of men. The deity bestowed on me the gift of a jewel like the planet Venus, and it was given unto me in my left hand, and thereby have I been enabled to determine the superior and inferior among Buddhist sects and Scriptures in virtue of my perfect understanding of All the Scriptures. Above all, the Shingon Sect is destroying the truth of the Hokekyo. This is the most serious matter of all, therefore have I deferred for a while attacking the Shingon Sect by beginning first of all to point out the fallacies of the Zen and Nenbuts Sects. . . . Although I knew that I should be killed if I proclaimed and denounced it, yet, in order to acknowledge Kokuzo's kindness, I took it upon me to denounce all the fallacies, first of all, in front of a certain *Joen* and a few people at my master Dozen's service room facing south, in the precincts of the monastery of Kiyosumi, in *Tojo* of Awa province, on 28th of April in the fifth year of Kencho, etc." (Works, pp. 793–4).

He, without doubt, got many opponents here, especially the lord of this district, *Kagenobu of Tojo,* got furiously angry with him and wanted to kill him on the spot, for he hated Nichiren ever so deeply, but he was prevented by Dozen. According to another letter of his, it is written as follows :

" I in no wise dreaded propagating this law, although my parents opposed me by their wild gesticulations, and even my previous master disowned me, etc." (Works, p. 868 ; see *ibid.*, pp. 39–40, 713).

Nichiren started for Kamakura on missionary work and he founded a cell at *Matsbagayats of Nagoe* in Kamakura. He was looking out for a good opportunity there.

4.   WARNING AND THE FIRST EXILE

At the outset, he was used to going out to preach his new doctrine on one of the cross-roads named *Komachi*, which was one of the gayest places in Kamakura. Sometimes he preached the truth of the Hokekyo, sometimes he denounced Buddhist fallacies, and sometimes he would criticize politics, etc. A crowd of people always surrounded him. Most of them turned

persecutors on the spot, whīle some took advantage
of the extraordinary instruction. He was now hated
by almost all the citizens. He was stoned, he was
beaten with sticks, he was abused every day whenever
he appeared before the public.

At that time people were panic-stricken by famines,
comets, fearful epidemics and earthquakes, etc.,
which followed one another incessantly. The miserable
condition was such that people could hardly bear to
look at it. Nichiren pondered over what might be
the root of these calamities, so he went to the library
of the *Zisso* temple not very far from Kamakura in
order to reread all the Scriptures.

He wrote an essay in order to get his idea into shape
and entitled it " Rissho Ankoku Ron." It is written
in a flowery style with care for rhetoric and much more
dialogue in the original than in the following translation.
The title means " The Establishment of Righteousness
for the Security of the Country." (The Japanese
Emperor conferred an honourable title on Nichiren as
The Great Master Risshō on the thirteenth of October
in the eleventh year of Taisho, A.D. 1922).

It begins thus :

" A visitor came forth unto me bewailing that :
From a few years ago to this very day, there have
been calamities and catastrophies in heaven and in
earth, famines and plagues accompanied with misery
throughout the land. Horses and cattle are dying
on the roadsides, and the skeletons are scattered on
the road ; more than one-half of the population have
died, and there is no one who does not mourn it "
(Works, p. 1).

Out of compassion, not only for the sake of the people who were suffering as a result of these calamities, but also in consequence of the superstitious practices to which they resorted, Nichiren turned the question over in his mind and exclaimed : What are the causes of these evils, and how can they be remedied ? After examining All the Scriptures, especially the significant letters of those Scriptures, viz. the *Konkōmyokyo* (Śuvarṇa Prabhāsa), *Daishukkyo*, *Ninnōkyo*, *Yakushikyo* (Bheṣajyaguru-sūtra), etc., he considered the causes of these calamities. As a result, he reached the final conclusion that these calamities were caused by the people's negligence of the righteousness of the Hokekyo. Thereupon he described with the authority of the Scriptures what he thought, in other words he gave his ardent warnings in his powerful letters. The calamities are nothing but a great warning from heaven to human beings concerning their adhesion to heresy ; so he believed. Thus he sent this essay to the Hojos Government, and also laid it before the public. He prophesied in this book. According to it, if the Government and the nation would not turn to the Truth of the Hokekyo, the country would experience foreign invasions and internal disturbances (Works, p. 19). He presented this essay to the Government authorities on the 16th day in the seventh month of 1260. But most of the authorities of the Government were the believers or converts of the Zen or Nenbuts Sects, and they were influenced by some other priests who were opponents of Nichiren. The Government ignored his warning and said nothing openly about it, while they tacitly permitted the people's plot of attack on Nichiren's life ; not only the

K

common people, but even men of honour and high position joined together.

Suddenly an enveloping attack on his cell was carried out by a mob which was composed of several thousand men who were, of course, the sectarian opponents. Fortunately he escaped the jaws of death and left Kamakura for a while and visited one of his supporters, Lord *Toki*, who lived in the *Shimōsa* province. The Government had promulgated the constitution which is admired as an ideal law by historians. To form any faction is strictly prohibited in that constitution, nevertheless the sectarianism of the Government authorities led them to turn a deaf ear to a great criminal action which happened in the very seat of the Government. Nichiren writes :

" On the occasion of the great earthquake I wrote a book which I presented to the late lay-priest of the *Saimyōji* (i.e. Hojo Tokiyori, who resided in the Saimyōji temple). Nonetheless he did not ask me (about the warning in the Rissho Ankoku Ron) nor did he adopt it. People might have thought they would not be punished even if they injured Nichiren, because he was the man hated by the Government ; thereupon monks and laymen of the Nenbuts Sect, with some honourable men of high position at their back, resolved to attack me. At midnight, my small cell was attacked by a crowd of several thousands, but how good fortune favoured me, for I had a narrow escape from injury. But its carrying out had been previously agreed upon between the Government and the people, therefore none of the mob was punished and the weighty statecraft was broken. Afterwards they were surprised to find me still alive, and exiled me to the province of *Izu*. It seems that they did not ascribe the cause of their sins to excess of hatefulness for the other man, and further, they dared to break the constitution themselves " (Works, pp. 552–3 ; cp. *ibid.*, pp. 592–3).

During his stay with the Lord Toki, it is said that he preached his religion a hundred times to the people and several souls were converted to his view. Soon after he resolved to appear in Kamakura again at the risk of his precious life. From a psychological point of view it can be said that his own conviction of the Buddha's prophecy began to be fervent from now onward. Of course, there are a few letters to demonstrate his earlier conviction, for instance, those few lines of his " On the master, teacher and parents " (Works, pp. 1149–50) are one authority concerning the above. He wrote a letter one day to one of his disciples in which he says :

" It is sure that the practitioner of the Hokekyo will appear. For the more he will encounter great troubles, the more he will confirm his joy in his faith. A man who is free from great troubles is not the practitioner of the Hokekyo " (Works, p. 949).

He kept on attacking every kind of Buddhism every day more and more ever since he returned to Kamakura. The Government authorities and *Ryōkan of the Gokurakuji, Dōryū of the Kenchōji* and *Ryōchū of the Kōmyōji* (famous priests at that time and the severest opponents of Nichiren) acted in unison and set on foot an agitation for his expulsion. It must be borne in mind that the Shikken, the head of the Government authorities at that time, was *Hojo Nagatoki*. On the other hand, the temple Gokurakuji was established by Hojo *Shigetoki*, who was the father of the then Shikken, Nagatoki. The father and son and their family were converts of Ryokan, who was created the abbot of the temple in favour with them. And then Ryokan was the severest opponent of Nichiren. These were the relationships, therefore Nichiren was exiled to Izu without a trial which ought to have taken place according to the regulation of the constitution. Even the Hojos, who had the reputation of being honourable and just, were blind where sectarianism was concerned. Nichiren describes it as follows :

" For no reason whatsoever Nagatoki, the son of Shigetoki of the Gokurakuji, exiled me to the province of Izu, being in sympathy with his father " (Works, p. 593).

From this fact we can gather the real circumstances of the event. He was sent under guard to Izu by sea from the shore (Yuigahama) of Kamakura on the twelfth day of May, A.D. 1261, and landed at *Kawana*, where he was fortunately taken into safety by a fisherman called *Hunamori Yasaburo*. The Government had published an official notice about Nichiren to the effect that nobody should protect him. The fisherman was, of course, aware of this, nevertheless when he beheld the poor monk who looked unhappy on the shore, he could not help taking him into safety out of pity and kindheartedness. He reasoned with his wife and they agreed to protect Nichiren from troubles and to prevent him from being seen. How deeply did Nichiren feel gratitude amongst the thorns in this place of exile! It is obvious in the following paragraphs of his letter to Yasaburo :

"I am very much obliged to you for sending a messenger expressly, and with thanks I received *Chimaki* (a boiled rice-dumpling in bamboo wrapping), wine, sun-dried rice, pepper, and paper. Your messenger gave your message that I had better keep these things secret, which I well understood. As you know, I, Nichiren, was exiled here on last 12th of May and arrived at this port. When during my torture on the shore, you kindly took care of me, although I had not yet heard your name. I wonder what unconscious understanding there was in you! It seems to me like a man who was a practitioner of the Hokekyo in the past, reborn as a Yasaburo of Hunamori in the Latter Days and protecting me, Nichiren.

"Such generosity may sometimes be offered by man, but how extremely I admired your wife's kind devotion to me! And especially how after thirty odd days, you inclined your minds by degrees to the faith and thereby supported me, how marvellous it is! I am hated to excess by the lord of the district and people much more than by Kamakura. People are looking daggers at me whenever they see me, and are also full of abuse.

"Now, rice must be scarce in May as usual, but nevertheless you have sustained me, oh! may I believe that my, Nichiren's, parents are reborn here, as you at Kawana of Ito in Izu province " (Works, p. 953. According to a paragraph in this letter,

Nichiren sent a letter to him previously, but it has not been found yet).

Under their respectful protection, Nichiren again began his propagation here, in his very place of exile. The lord of the district hated Nichiren in the beginning, but occasionally when the lord fell ill he sent his messenger for Nichiren in order to ask him to pray for his recovery. So at last, the lord presented Nichiren with a standing image of Buddha. Nichiren ever after kept this Buddha's image by his side wherever he went.

At the beginning of the following year, Nichiren wrote an essay on his impression of his exile and sent it to one of his followers, Lord *Kudo*. The essay is called " On the fourfold Indebtedness." According to this essay, he received two deep impressions of his exile ; on the one hand he was extremely glad of the exile as a result of the persecution on account of his propagation ; and on the other hand he was distressed about the sins of his opponents, who were the cause of his good fortune in becoming the practitioner of the Hokekyo owing to their persecution. In order to become the practitioner of the Hokekyo, he must naturally have such opponents, hence his benevolent sorrow. Moreover, there is written in the essay much more important matter about his confessing his conviction of the prophesied man, though he had not yet said so conclusively. It is as follows :

" I, Nichiren, do not keep the Buddhist commandments bodily, nor am I delivered from the three (mental) viruses, yet, nevertheless I took great care of daily matters, by doing so I thought I might be able to deepen my faith and might give opportunities to others with reference to the Hokekyo. Even married monks are respected by people, and there are some monks who dared to eat meat in the Latter Days (the Buddhist commandments prohibit these actions by monks and nuns, but they are out of practice in the present day with a few exceptions). But I, Nichiren, am not married in any sense, nor do I eat meat. Without having a wife and children I won ill fame as a lawless priest, and again, without killing even an insect, my name is tarnished all over the country. It may have been more than in the case of the Buddha Shakamuni, who had been abused by several kinds of heathens. This, indeed, is a result of devil's jealousy on account of my right faith in accordance with the instruction of the Hokekyo, to which faith everybody was less devoted than myself. Nevertheless, in spite of my being the lowly, ignorant and lawless, I have been prophesied to meet with persecution in the Hokekyo by the Buddha over 2000 years ago, the truth of which words cannot express sufficiently. There have elapsed some twenty-four or five years since I began to study, but it is only for these six or seven years that I have fully believed in the Hokekyo. Though I believed in it, I was prevented from fully practising it owing to my laziness and also to study and affairs in general ; and thus all that I could read was one chapter or one volume or often a mere utterance of the Sacred Title in a whole day.

"On the contrary, now, I believe I practise the Hokekyo ceaselessly throughout the twenty-four hours every day and night, during those two hundred and forty odd days from the twelfth of May last year to the sixteenth of the first month of the current year. Because my present condition was caused through my propagation of the Hokekyo, it can be said therefore that I have read and practised the Hokekyo all hours of the day, even when walking, standing, resting or lying. I cannot think of greater happiness than this for human life. Behold! there might exist a man seeking salvation voluntarily who might hope for a happy future life ; and for the sake of such a desire, he might make an effort by snatches. Now, for my part, though I do not think of, nor have read of the Scripture, I dare say I am practising the Hokekyo, am I not ? " (Works, pp. 420–2).

The reader will be able to see the furtherance of his conviction of Honge Jogyo in the above lines, but it must be noticed that he did not proclaim that he was the Honge Jogyo so far as the wording is concerned. In the following month, he systematized and proclaimed his Five Critical Principles (Works, pp. 262–3) which we have already explained in the previous chapter. Of course, we can imagine that the system of the Five Critical Principles were conceived by him previously. But he could not announce it before his exile, for not even one of the prophecies was yet realized. He announced all his important thoughts and words step by step in proportion to the degree of his realization.

He stayed at the place of exile for three calendar years and was released on the 22nd in the second month of 1263. There were some reasons behind this ; for instance, Shigetoki died, probably insane, in November, 1261, the same year as Nichiren's exile, and Tokiyori (the lay-priest of the Saimyoji) very often suffered from nightmares (Works, p. 553 ; cp. Works (the Ryogonkaku edition), Second Series, p. 91). But let us omit these minute events.

After a while, Nichiren returned to Kamakura, where many followers were anxiously awaiting him. After his return to Kamakura many more violent attacks were made (Works, p. 554).

5. SWORD-CUT IN THE PINE FOREST

Nichiren's mother's illness was announced to him in the eighth month, 1264. He left Kamakura for his native village as soon as he received the news. But, alas, when he reached his mother's cottage, it seemed as if she had passed away. He was grieved over his mother and prayed to Heaven for her recovery, and fortunately his mother revived from the syncope by his aid ; day and night, thereupon, he nursed his sick mother without intermission. She recovered and lived four years more. He writes :

" With my prayer my loving mother not only was cured, but lived for four years longer " (Works, p. 811).

On this occasion of his return home he arranged with his former old master, Dozen, to hold a meeting, but Nichiren, who was under the lord Kagenobu's surveillance, could not see his former master in the monastery. Therefore, they met at another place near his native home. When Nichiren saw Dozen after twelve years' absence, he gave him his kindly advice, first of all, hoping to make a true Buddhist of him. Without compunction Nichiren pointed out the master's turbulence regarding the Hokekyo and remonstrated with him both in sentiment and reason. Of course, he thought that he had better speak without provocation and courteously, but he changed his mind and reasoned with him as he thought fit, for he knew that now his master was an elderly man and that he might die at any moment, and, moreover, they might probably not see each other again. Therefore Nichiren ventured to speak his mind without any circumlocution. All Nichiren's earnest endeavours to instruct fell like water off a duck's back. However, Nichiren's instruction turned out to be of some value in later days. Nichiren exclaimed, " Now I can answer for the master's grace " (Works, pp. 1544–5 and 357–8).

It happened on the 14th of October, and Nichiren went to see the Lord Kudo on the 11th of the following month. On the way there, he was suddenly attacked in the pine forest, which is named *Komatsbara*, by several hundred men-at-arms under the command of Tojo Kagenobu, the lord of that district. As the plan on which Kagenobu had been engaged for a long time past had matured, he seized this opportunity. Two disciples of Nichiren had been killed and others wounded. Just then the Lord Kudo came to the place with his few retainers to welcome him. As soon as the Lord Kudo reached the shambles, he cut his way into the enemy and slashed in all directions, but he could not resist the heavy odds, so he, too, died fighting bravely. Now, Kagenobu spurred a horse on Nichiren in order to kill him in a single attack.   But how fortunate Nichiren was! for he escaped from the jaws of death, although wounded on the forehead.   Nichiren described it in his letter to Lord Nanjo on the 13th of the twelfth month of the same year.   It said :

" We were ambushed by several hundred men of the Nenbuts Sect on the road of the pine forest of Tojo in the Awa province, in the twilight, on the 11th of November of this year.   I was accompanied by some ten disciples, of whom only three or four were stalwart men.   Showers of arrows poured on us and the clashing of swords flashed like lightning.   One of my disciples was killed on the spot, two others were severely wounded, and I myself was also struck and so slashed (on the forehead) that it seemed I was killed, but I had a miraculous escape, though how I cannot explain. My faith in the Hokekyo has ever since increased. In the fourth volume of the Scripture, Buddha says : Even at the present day of Buddha's being, there happened many cases of grudge and jealousy, how much more in the days after His Death ! (Yamakawa, p. 327 ; Kern, p. 219).   And again, in the fifth volume, it says : It is very difficult to believe on account of the hatred of all the people, etc. (Yamakawa, p. 418 ; Kern, p. 275).   Very many students read and learn the Hokekyo.   But no one has been wounded for having propagated the Scripture, but there are many who have been beaten for adultery or theft.   Therefore, all readers of this Scripture in Japan are merely nominal, but they have not yet read these words of the Scripture.   Only I, Nichiren, alone have read it.   My case corresponds to ' I do not love, nor am I heedful of my body and life, but I heed only the Supreme Truth ' (Yamakawa, p. 392 ; Kern, pp. 260–1). Now, without any doubt, I, Nichiren, am the Sole Practitioner of the Hokekyo in Japan " (Works, p. 281).

He thus for the first time proclaimed himself to be the *sole practitioner of the Hokekyo in Japan*. The Lord Kudo's posthumous son, in later days, served Nichiren as one of his disciples in obedience, to his father's will. After this danger, it is said that Nichiren went away on a mission for about four years and returned to Kamakura in the beginning of the fifth year of Bunnei, 1271.

6. His Eleven Letters

At that time the Mongol conquerors who had spread over the Asiatic continent had nearly been subjugated. The Mongol was planning the conquest of Japan by way of Korea. Nine years elapsed since Nichiren had sent his warning to the Government. Suddenly an envoy from Kubrai, the Mongol King, was deputed to Japan in an early month in 1271. There was a national panic, and express messengers kept flying to and fro between Kyoto and Kamakura, viz. the Court and the Government. Nichiren must not allow the opportunity to slip by. He met one of the government authorities to whom he gave a warning. As soon as he reached home, he wrote an interpretation of the said warning, " Rissho Ankoku Ron," which had been sent to the government nine years ago (Works, pp. 426–7).

Moreover, he wrote a letter (Works, p. 428) to another official in order to accelerate his warning. But nothing came of it. Hereupon, he resorted to a last expedient, that is, he sent his letters to eleven men who were specially selected for the purpose, four politicians and seven priests. He expressed himself in different ways, taking into consideration the receivers' character, position and existing relation with him. All the letters conveyed the following signification.

" Let us all gather at some place as quickly as possible and confront one another. I am expecting and longing for it ever so much, but I do not by any means disdain all the sects."

He sent the Eleven Letters (Works, pp. 429–38) after preparing for death. The following, which was sent to his disciples and adherents simultaneously, expresses the fact in an eloquent manner.

" Subsequent to the coming of the Mongolian envoy, I despatched eleven letters to various officials and prelates. Prosecution is sure to be the lot of myself, Nichiren, as also of my followers, and exile or death will be our sentence. Be resigned to your fate. Remonstrances of a vigorous nature were intentionally made, for no other reason than to arouse the people. All is anticipated by me, Nichiren, with the utmost composure. Do not worry about your wives or children, nor about your households ; do not be scared when confronting the authorities. Avail yourselves of this your opportunity to be released from Births and Deaths, and to attain the fruits of Buddhahood, etc. " (Works, p. 439).

But his letters were ignored and no response to them was made. There are some interesting reasons which, however, may be omitted here.

Japan again received a second notification in March of the following year, and again the Mongol sent messengers to Japan in the ninth month of the same year. Nichiren thereupon wrote letters to the eleven people in order to press them for answers to the letters which he had sent the previous year. This time a few of them sent answers to Nichiren, and it seemed that matters had become smooth for him while he was expecting fresh developments (Works, p. 440 ; Satomi, " New Study of Nichirenism," pp. 105–6).

He describes the position thus :

" It seems strange to me that I have never since received any intimation from the Government, while I have been prepared for death or exile because of the bitterest warning which I had given. . . . I was exiled once for the reason of my propagation of the Hokekyo. Now, what a disappointment it is that I am not condemned to death. I have made endeavours, hoping that such an event might happen, and I sent strong remonstrances to various authorities. My age, now, has reached the fiftieth year ; should I be spared much longer, let me devote my life, which is liable to be wasted in an uncultivated field, to the Perfect Truth of the Hokekyo " (Works, p. 440 ; cf. pp. 744–6, 968).

7. The Sentence of Death

The following year, 1274, came round while circumstances had not caused rapid progress in consequence of his Eleven Letters. Spring had departed and summer had arrived. The country had suffered from a long continuous drought which brought hardships to the farmers and all the people. Then, Ryokan, the priest of the Gokurakuji began to pray for rain with the support of the people's hopes. On this occasion, Nichiren sent his message to Ryokan urging him to judge whether their laws were right or wrong. Nichiren said, " If with your prayers you can cause it to rain within a week, then shall I gladly be one of your disciples, and if you cannot make it rain, then you shall be my follower." Ryokan acquiesced and began to pray for rain from the 18th of June to the 24th of the same month. Not only the drought continued for several weeks in spite of Ryokan's endeavours, but into the bargain the suffering of the people was intensified from day to day with hurricanes. Hereupon, Nichiren sent him a messenger bidding him come and see Nichiren and learn how to act to attain Buddhahood, and how to bring about a rainfall. Ryokan stamped with mortification (Works, pp. 571–2, 547, 395).

Now, by the way, let us get a brief idea about Ryokan's character. He was the abbot of the Gokurakuji, as I have already stated. He was revered by the people, and especially by the nobility. He was regarded also as an incarnation of the Buddha owing to his care for the sick and miserable. But, he was an extremely crafty person, and he was accustomed to use subtle expedients whenever he opposed Nichiren's connection with religion. Nichiren's sharp eyes stigmatized him as such, hence his scathing satires on Ryokan's character in several letters (see Works).

Ryokan, who had a bitter experience through his prayers for rain, was having his revenge for his failure. Now it happened on the 8th of July that Nichiren received a letter from a priest called *Gyōbin*, who wrote to Nichiren in his letter that he wished to come face to face with him (Works, p. 442). In reply Nichiren wrote on the 13th :

" I beg respectfully to acknowledge the receipt of your several questions, but I regret to inform you that I cannot agree to a private controversy with you, which you had better report to the government, and on your obtaining an official sanction, we could discuss what is right and what is wrong. It will very much gratify me " (Works, p. 442).

Now, Ryokan gathered a number of ill-disposed priests together and presented a petition to the government with their joint signatures. This petition stigmatized Nichiren's attack on all the sects as being disorderly, and they fabricated a tale to the effect that Nichiren had accumulated weapons in his hut ; not only that, they also slandered Nichiren, saying he had burnt or thrown into the river the images of Amita Buddha, which were the object of their worship. And, they concluded the letter by saying :

" We sincerely hope we may uplift righteousness by destroying Nichiren's heresy and confronting him as speedily as possible " (Works, p. 443).

Accordingly the government conveyed that letter to Nichiren and commanded him to reply. He attempted first of all to refute the Buddhist doctrine, and then vehemently defeated their plan of fabrications (Works, pp. 444–5).

There was no reason for punishing him, for Nichiren's answer was so sensible ; so it was an utter failure. But now Ryokan contrived a second plot, viz. by working himself into the favour of the court-ladies, who were fervent believers in Ryokan himself. Thus, they plotted a conspiracy with the aid of the court-ladies. As a result Nichiren was at last summoned to court on the tenth (perhaps) of the ninth month, and he was tried by *Hei no Saemon*, the major-domo of the Hojos. Apropos, Hei no Saemon had, at that time, one and all at his back, and he was besides an enthusiastic adherent of Amita Buddhism, he was also one of the bitterest opponents of Nichiren.

Such being the circumstances, Nichiren was tried. He gave his answers to the questions clearly one by one, and thus describes his attitude :

" It was after all out of their depth, so these fellows of the Nenbuts, etc., ingratiated themselves with the court-ladies and feigned reasons purporting that Nichiren had boldly proclaimed many things, such as, for instance, that the late lay-priest of the Saimyoji and the late lay-priest of the Gokurakuji had been sent into the Nethermost hell ; or, such as : lay into ashes those great temples, the *Kenchoji*, the *Jufukuji*, the *Chorakuji*, the *Daibutsji*, etc. ; or, such as : cut off the heads of priests, Doryu, Ryokan and so forth Consequently the government decided that Nichiren

L

must not be acquitted in any circumstances, so it was decided that Nichiren should be summoned to court. So I went. Then a commissioner told me that a report was made to the government such as the above. Therefore, I affirmed that certainly I did say so, but what I am supposed to have said is a bare-faced lie, viz. that the lord of Saimyoji and the lord of Goku-rakuji fell into hell. I did not say such a thing at all immediately after their death, but I gave and am still continuing to give my warning to them from the very day of their life. In short, such warnings of mine as the above were given out of patriotism. If you wish to rule the country calmly, let me be confronted by the authorities together with all the priests. And if without just cause the government punish me on behalf of the priests, will not the country regret having done so in later days ? If the government is arrogant enough to listen to the messenger of the Buddha, then I shall be punished. Within one hundred days or one year or three years, or for certain within seven years after my exile or death, fighting will take place among those of the same family of the Hojos, and afterwards the country will be attacked by foreign invasions, especially by the western country. You will be regertful then.

"Thus did I speak to Hei no Saemon, but alas ! he rushed and shouted in a frenzied way regardless of people, so much so that we could imagine the *Dajōnyūdō* to be mad " (Works, pp. 393–4).

In the early morning, two days later, Nichiren sent to Hei no Saemon his letter with his essay " Rissho Ankoku Ron," in which he says :

" I was very pleased to see you yesterday. . . . I was prevented by the false charge and slanderous reports of the heresies so that I could not attain my aim, in spite of having been very loyal for these long years, while I should have been praised for my wisdom of the Law and for my patriotism. I am so sorry it was so very difficult to instruct you, because it was my impression when I saw you that you were in a very violent temper " (Works, p. 447).

When he despatched his letter to Hei no Saemon, the course to be pursued by the government towards Nichiren had already been decided upon. Probably soon after reading this letter Hei no Saemon in person set off to seize Nichiren, and he was in command of about three hundred armed soldiers under *Shobo's* guidance, who was one of Nichiren's disciples, and whom we may compare with Judas who betrayed Christ. All of a sudden, the troops broke into Nichiren's hut and destroyed whatever came within their reach (Works, pp. 529–30, 394). Nichiren did not show the least agitation, but exclaimed in a loud voice :

" How strange is the madness of Hei no Saemon ! Behold ! You are now going to let the Pillar of Japan fall " (Works, p. 394).

Further he describes the spectacle :

" I, Nichiren, would seem to be very much threatened because I incurred the Lord's displeasure ; for, having acted quite contrary to their expectation ; the soldiers might have thought my action unendurable, and their countenances fell " (Works, p. 394).

Suddenly Shobo, who betrayed his master, approached Nichiren and snatched away one roll of the Hokekyo which Nichiren held in his hand, and with it struck Nichiren in the face. As chance would have it, the roll was the fifth volume of the Hokekyo, in which the Buddha prophesied terrible persecutions for Honge Jogyo in the Latter Days. Nichiren writes :

" Shobo struck me with the roll of the fifth volume of the Hokekyo. The stick with which he struck me was the fifth volume, and it was also the fifth volume which prophesied that the practitioner of the Hokekyo in the days of the Latter Law should be struck by his opponent. How marvellous this Scripture is ! But when I was beaten by him in the presence of many people I was mortified, because I, too, am a man, and I would have snatched that roll back from him and torn it into pieces if it had been in my power to do so. But, oh, it was the fifth volume of the Hokekyo. If I could only attain the fruits of Buddhahood, I should not forget his kindness, how much more that of the Hokekyo " (Works, p. 602).

Nichiren often made mention of it to the end of his life. At any rate they fetched Nichiren and made him ride bareback, exposed to the public gaze, through the city of Kamakura, just as if he were a rebel (Works, p. 529). Afterwards they led Nichiren to the office where they put him on formal trial in the evening of the same day. He announced what he thought openheartedly without the slightest hesitation. He says:

" They sometimes roared with laughter and sometimes they lost their temper while I reasoned in detail with Hei no Saemon about the evils of the Shingon Sect, the Zen Sect and the Nenbuts Sect, and about the cause of the failure of Ryokan and his prayer for rain, in the very evening of the twelfth day " (Works, p. 394).

Trampling upon their own constitution and the government, and regardless of Nichiren's statement, they sentenced him to banishment to the island of Sado in the North Sea. He states :

" It was reported to the world as being exile, but was in reality decided that I should be secretly put to death " (Works, p. 554 ; cf. *ibid.*, pp. 449, 145, 554–5, 572).

On this occasion also Nichiren gave his strict instructions to all his disciples and adherents, which were to the following effect.

" Every one of you, my disciples, if you are proud of being my disciples, must not be afraid. Worry not about your parents, family, or households. From eternity to the present day the people who have thrown away their lives for their parents, for their children or their households, were and are more numerous than the dust on the earth, while no one has died a martyr for the sake of the Truth of the Hokekyo. Although some may have appeared to be practitioners of strong conviction, none the less when they met with persecution, they retrograded and yielded. . . .

" Prepare, all ye my disciples ! To change our bodies into the Hokekyo is like changing stone into gold or changing excrement into rice. . . ." (Works, pp. 392–3).

But some of his disciples became traitors (Works, pp. 613, 1075). Nichiren rode to the place of execution. He alighted from his horse when he approached the gate of the Hachiman shrine, the seat of national worship, and he spoke in a loud voice :

" Oh, Hachiman ! Art Thou in truth a Divine Being ? . . . When the Great Master Dengyo preached on the Hokekyo, didst Thou not do homage to him by laying at his feet a gown of purple colour. I now say unto Thee that I am the Only One whose life is the Hokekyo. There is no fault in me whatsoever ; I am proclaiming the Truth, for the sole purpose of saving the people who dwell in the land from sinking into the deepest of Hells on account of degrading the Hokekyo. If it came to pass that this land were subjugated by the Mongols, wouldst Thou, O Hachiman, alone with the Sungoddess be in safety ? Let me now say unto Thee that when our Lord Shakamuni preached the Hokekyo, all the Buddhas gathered together from ten quarters, like unto a sun and a sun, a moon and a moon, stars and stars, mirrors and mirrors, and were ranged face to face with one another ; and with hosts of heaven within their midst, deities and saints of India, China, Japan, etc., present in the congregation, all of them vowed to watch over those who should labour to perpetuate the Hokekyo.
" Now shouldst Thou come hither and fulfil what Thou has sworn. Why then comest Thou not to fulfil Thy Promise ! When, I, Nichiren, this night, shall have been beheaded and shall have passed away to the Paradise of Vulture Peak, I shall declare unto Our Lord Shakamuni that Thou, Hachiman, and the

Sungoddess have not fulfilled the vows. Therefore, if Thou fearest, tarry not, but do Thy duty ! " (Works, pp. 395–6).

He rode on again, looking askance at the guardian soldiers and busybodies. And again, when he approached the Shrine of *Goryo*, which stands near the sea-coast, he spoke to the guard, " I have a message to send to one of my disciples here " (Works, p. 396), and he sent his page to Shijo Kingo. He ran up on hearing Nichiren's message with his three brothers (this suggests that the course of the government was rapidly pursued and in great secrecy). Nichiren told them :

" Now, I am going to be beheaded this night. It is the very thing for which I have been longing for these several years " (Works, p. 396 ; cp. p. 451).

He followed Nichiren along the road together with his brothers and Nichiren arrived at *Tats no Kuchi* at midnight, which was illuminated with watch-fire. Now, everything is ready for his execution. Clasping his hands, Nichiren sat down on the seat awaiting the downward stroke of the sword. Suddenly Shijo Kingo burst into tears and expressed his thousand sensations in a word, making ready to follow Nichiren to death :

" Farewell, O now is the time ! "

With a cry of encouragement, Nichiren spoke :

" What a negligent man you are ! Smile at such a delight. Why don't you keep your promise of long standing " (Works, p. 396).

All of a sudden, the sky was ablaze with light, he writes :

" Something bright like a ball of fire, like the moon (cf. Works, pp. 593, 451) appeared in the direction of *Enoshima*, and it flew from the south-east to the north-west, and everyone's face was visible. The swordsman turned dizzy and fell into a swoon ; the soldiers were panic-stricken and ran some one hundred yards away, some squatted down on the ground, others prostrated themselves on horseback " (Works, pp. 396–7).

Further, he continues :

" I, Nichiren, spoke to them : Why do ye flee from such a criminal person of the blackest dye ! But no one came nigh despite my calling : Come hither ! Come nearer ! Again, I urged them, saying : Day is dawning, hasten to behead me, if so be your purpose, before your dishonourable behaviour shines in the rising sun ! But for a while there was no response " (Works, pp. 396–7).

Thus the execution was miraculously baffled by the awful signs of Heaven's displeasure. An express messenger from the government arrived, and re-prieved the victim. Nichiren was sent to *Echi* in the morning of the 13th. He was there in the custody of *Honma Rokurō* awaiting a new sentence. Some soldiers of the guard became his converts. Late the following night the messenger from the government came to Echi sentencing him to be exiled to Sado.

On the 21st Nichiren sent a letter to Shijo, it said :

" Tats no Kuchi is the place where I, Nichiren, designed to die. The place, therefore, may be compared with a paradise ; because all happenings there were for the sake of the Hokekyo. . . . Verily, I say unto you that wherever dangers were confronted by Nichiren, there indeed is Buddha's land. . . . Verily, verily, when I am on Vulture Peak, there shall I speak unto Our Lord of your fidelity and willingness to follow me unto death " (Works, p. 451).

Nichiren expressed his heartfelt gladness to Shijo Kingo many and many times, so let us cite one more example.

" Again and again, I recall to mind, that you were following me when I was on my way to be beheaded, and that you sobbed and cried with a loud voice, holding my horse's bridle. How can I forget that as long as I live ? Should you descend into Hell because of your grave iniquities (accumulated), then would I in no wise be obedient to the call of my Lord the Buddha, however much He might summon me to Buddhahood, nay I would rather follow you to Hades. If it is your fate and mine to be in Hell, the Buddha Shakamuni and the Scripture will surely be there with us " (Works, pp. 750–7 ; cf. pp. 909, 900).

Let it be said, however, that the government seized many disciples of Nichiren and confined them in an underground dungeon for committing the crime of incendiarism which had really been the doings of Ryokan's gang (Works, p. 188).

8. The Exile To Sado

Nearly a month later on he, at last, had to go to Sado, an island in the snowy North Sea. He deeply commiserated his disciples who were in a dungeon below ground, and he sent a letter to *Nichiro* and others. It says:

" I, Nichiren, shall depart to the Province of Sado to-morrow. It is exceedingly cold this evening even here, how much more so over there in a dungeon ; yes, I think of you with sympathy, I am stricken with sadness. Oh, verily, you are the man who has read the Hokekyo both corporally and spiritually, therefore it is for you to save parents, relations and every being with your virtues. The other men who also read the Hokekyo only read it by word of mouth, not spiritually ; or read it spiritually, but not corporally. How honourable of you to have read it both corporally and spiritually ! I believe no more happenings will threaten you, inasmuch as the Scripture says :

> Heavens will send angels to them to succour them ; One might even attack them with the sword and rod, but without being able to harm them (Yamakawa, p. 422).

Hoping that when you are released from prison you will hasten to come, and we shall behold each other " (Works, p. 747 ; this letter is dated the 9th of the 10th month).

On the tenth of October, Nichiren left Echi for the Isle of Sado, which, at that time, was the place of exile for life. He arrived at *Teradomari*, a haven, in the province of *Echigo*. He spent a week there, for the gale raged. During his stay there he carried his thoughts back to the past for old sake's sake. And at last he sent a letter to Lord Toki to express his thousand sensations. The letter is called " The Letter from Teradomari," which is counted as one of his important letters. In it, he says :

" I, Nichiren, have been banished many and many times and exiled twice. The Hokekyo proclaims the truth which is universal, and for all ages, for the past, as well as for the present, and for the future. What it declares concerning the past in the 20th chapter, Sadāparibhūta, is true of to-day as it is revealed in the 13th chapter, Perseverance, and vice versa. . . .

" There exist at the present time the three kinds who are antagonistic to the Hokekyo. Should none of these eight billion million of saints be manifest, it would be as unnatural as an ebb not being succeeded by a flow, or the waning moon by the crescent. Moonlight is reflected in clear water, birds make a tree their abode as long as there is life in it. I, Nichiren, am the shepherd who tends these saints who number eight billion million, and it is they who protect him " (Works, p. 457, and see the Scripture, Cap. 13 and 20, Kern, 12 and 19).

Moreover he added in the last line :

" Exceedingly do I feel anxious about the prisoned disciples. Please give them all my hearty greetings on the very first opportunity."

Thus, his conviction gradually became firmly

realized. He was by order put into a dilapidated cell which stood in the snowy desert. He describes it thus :

" Since the first of November have I been dwelling here in the desert which was called *Tsukawara* in the background of *Rokuro Saemon's* House. The place is like unto *Rendaino*, the graveyard in Kyoto. There is, of course, no Buddha's image in my small cell of six feet square. The broken roof and walls admitting perpetual snow into my cell. I hung up the Buddha's image which I carried with me (from Kamakura. He got it at Izu during his first exile there) and I laid a fur-skin cushion on the bare floor and thus have I been spending my nights and days. It has snowed and hailed incessantly at nights, and the sun has not shone in the day time. What a lonely dwelling-place it is ! " (Works, p. 399).

On the 23rd he sent another letter to Lord Toki in which he wrote about his realized conviction more clearly. It says :

" During wellnigh two months since I have come to this Isle of Sado, bleak winds have been ever blowing, and although snowfall is sometimes intermittent the light of the Sun is always hidden from my sight. My body is impregnated with *the cold* (lit. felt the eight cold hells). In accordance with what I have written to you on the tenth of October, there have arisen, during the two thousand and two hundred years since Buddha's Death, various masters. . . . Tendai and Dengyo, the Great Masters, made the purport of the Truth explicit, nevertheless there remained one thing,

the most important law, which was not being propagated, and which law had been enacted in this
country. Did I, Nichiren, not fulfil my task ? And
there are already omens now which are more manifest
than at any time in the past. The Scripture says :
There appeared four leaders, Honge Jogyo, etc."

He concluded the letter with the following con-
solatory words :

" You must not lament over my exile. . . . Life is
short, you must not fear to die. After all, we ought
to long for the land of Buddha " (Works, p. 460).

For the first time, he combined his own personality
with that of Honge Jogyo. In icy cold, he spent every
day and night in meditation after recalling his severe
persecutions and pondering over his unique system of
philosophy of religion which must now be established,
as a matter of course, owing to his fulfilment of the
prophecy.

On the other hand, one day his religious opponents,
who dwelt in the districts of Sado, etc., congregated
and debated concerning Nichiren to the effect that :

" The notorious character, Nichiren, the enemy of
Amita Buddha and of all the beings, is exiled here.
There was never an example, before, of any one who
being exiled to this island was afterwards released
during his life ; and nobody was ever punished who
killed a prisoner in this island. Just now, as chance
would have it, he is living alone in the cemetery of
Tsukawara. However strong and mighty he is, he
lives alone, so we must attack him and kill him ; " or :

" Let the Lord of the district kill him," etc. (Works, pp. 400–1).

A decision was finally arrived at, and the deputation went to the Lord's office and stated their view. The following words were the Lord's answer :

" The addendum concerning Nichiren is handed to me to the effect that great care must be taken of him. If any accident through carelessness happens to him, the responsibility devolves on me. Therefore you had better attack him by reason of the Buddhist doctrine " (Works, p. 401).

There was a controversy early the following year. Of course, being without a rival, they were defeated *just as a melon would be split in twain by a sharp blade* (Works, pp. 401–2). When the controversy ended, the lord, Honma Rokuro, was called and stopped by Nichiren and told that wars were taking place among the Hojos, so he was advised to go to the seat of the government in order to join the official army. And Nichiren spoke :

" Even the Sungoddess and Hachiman shall make vows, joining hands, and shall adore me, Nichiren. Because I am the messenger from the Buddha Shaka-muni. . . . The people may even listen to me, Nichiren, but if it is the case that they wrongly respect me, then shall the country indeed be ruined. How much more then their hatred towards me, yes, towards me, who was also twice exiled. There is no doubt that this country would go to ruin but for my prayers for its salvation. As long as I pray it is calm in this country, nevertheless it is the fate of this country to incur punishment for illicit excess " (Works, p. 403).

After this controversy, *Sairen, Abuts* and his wife, and the lord of the district became his converts. Abuts was a warrior who had come here in attendance on the ex-Emperor, who had been sent to this island some half a century ago by the Hojos government after the Shokyu War. Abuts was a strong believer in Amita Buddhism, so that he determined to kill Nichiren, the antagonist of the Nenbuts Sect. But he was converted by Nichiren. Afterwards he and his wife supplied Nichiren with food with the sincerest heart, and they remained to the last. In the later days, Nichiren sent his heartfelt expression of gratitude. He writes in a letter to Abuts' wife as under :

" When I was exiled to Sado. . . . Setting aside for the moment Heaven's Mercy, how can I forget your kindness in that you came often to supply me with food, in company with your beloved husband in the evenings, in spite of threats of the lords and the believers of the Nenbuts Sect, who were on the watch on the way thither, towards Tsukawara, for Nichiren's converts. I confess that I have seen my loving mother reborn in you " (Works, p. 772).

At this time, Nichiren gave two important essays to Sairen, who was an exiled priest of the Tendai Sect and had already become one of Nichiren's disciples. The two essays are : " The Heritage of the Sole Great Thing concerning Life and Death " (Works, pp. 677–9) and " The Oral Instruction on the Attainment of Buddhahood of Trees and Grasses " (Works, pp.

1293–4, and see Anesaki, Nichiren, the Buddhist Prophet, pp. 65–7).

Nichiren received a letter of queries from Sairen after the above two essays were despatched, and he wrote an answer to him on the 13th of April. He wrote to the following effect in the conclusion :

" I will make a promise as I am so exceedingly pleased, that if you are released and return to Kyoto, then even if the government will not release me, I will give my instructions to Heaven and the gods, and I, Nichiren, too, will go back to Kamakura and will write to you. Or, if I am released prior to you and return to Kamakura, I am sure that I will be able to let you go back home to Kyoto by reason of my powerful order to Heaven " (Works, p. 762).

So then, Nichiren must establish and express the climax of his religious experience. The famous article, " Opening the Eyes " (*Kaimoku-shŏ*), was then written. He says :

" The Human Being who was called Nichiren was beheaded (at Tats no Kuchi) on the midnight of the twelfth day of September last year. But, here, *his Soul* revived across the sea in the Island of Sado, and he composed this (Opening the Eyes) in the thick snow in February of the year following, and I am going to despatch it to my disciples, etc." (Works, p. 66).

Indeed, now, all the words concerning the Buddha's prophecy in the thirteenth chapter of the Scripture have been entirely realized by Nichiren. Now, it is evident that the signification of Nichiren's personality is quite different from that of the pre-Sado periods. Thus Nichiren, for the first time, can proclaim his true thought with the highest authority.   Therefore he says :

" The teachings which I have revealed before I was exiled to Sado must be likened to all the Buddhist Scriptures of pious imposition " (Works, p. 580).

Immediately after this instruction he announced ⠂

" I am now revealing to you all in secret concerning the Great Law from Sado.   After Buddha's Death, Kasho, Anan, Ryuju, Tenjin, Tendai, Myoraku, Dengyo, Gishin, all of them bore this Law in mind, but did not utter it at all.   Because the Buddha prohibited this Law to be spoken until the Age of the Latter Law should begin.   I, Nichiren, might not be the messenger, but still my time corresponds with that time.   Moreover, my understanding of the Law is exceedingly deep and sound, so that I am going to take a pioneer's task in proclaiming this Law until the sage shall appear.   But when this Law once appears, then, all the laws which have been preached by many a priest and scholar during the ages of the Right Law and Fanciful Law, shall be as if they were the stars after the rising of the Sun, or as if they were the common carpenters after the appearance of an expert. After this time, all influences, inspirations and effects of Buddha's images and priests in the temples and monasteries which were founded during the ages of the Right and Fanciful Laws, shall disappear and only this Great Law shall spread all over the world " (Works, pp. 580–1).

M

Hereupon, Nichiren wrote, first of all, about his own personality, viz. its signification, position and mission, etc. There appeared some traitors among his disciples at that time on account of Nichiren's circumstances. Some of them cast a reflection on him and others denounced him with a loud voice. The gist of their questions was whether Nichiren really was the predicted one, and if so, why was he exiled and persecuted so many times unaided by God. On this criticism, Nichiren discoursed as follows :

" Some men and women who seemed believers in me, now abandoned the Hokekyo, harbouring doubts in the face of such circumstances as those wherein Nichiren was placed ; not only that, but, thinking themselves wise, they gave me wrong instruction. How regrettable that those men and women will inhabit Hell longer than the believers of the Nenbuts Sect " (Works, p. 466).

He goes on to say :

" Although St. Nichiren is our master, his manner is too rough, well let us keep on with our propagation of the Hokekyo in a gentle manner. Such a saying resembles the glimmer of a firefly laughing at the sun and moon, or as if a hillock treated a high mountain slightingly, or as if a brook would disdain the Ocean, or as if a magpie jeered at a crane " (Works, pp. 466–7).

Simultaneously with these circumstances there was a movement among his disciples at Kamakura for the remission of Nichiren's exile. And he sent them a letter concerning the movement, which says :

" All of you must not lament even if I am not released from exile quickly. Surely Heaven restrains it. Whoever will exhibit his feelings for Nichiren's remission is an undutiful disciple. Each of you must keep this in mind " (Works, p. 469).

With such a spiritual preparation, Nichiren wrote " Opening the Eyes," in which he tried to interpret his own mission in the days of the Latter Law. Moreover, he established " Five Degrees of Comparison of the Whole Buddhism," which we have mentioned already. The essay begins in the following strain :

" There are three kinds of objects which every man shall revere, viz. the lord, the master and the parents " (Works, pp. 23–81).

Nichiren intended to unite religion and ethics into one by determining these three objects. Of course, he had to throw light upon the doubts and questions concerning himself, therefore, to begin with, he included the above topics. He writes therefore :

" But the Tathagata Shakamuni is a liar because of His *twenty stanzas* of ' Perseverance ' of the Hokekyo, unless I, Nichiren, am born in this country (and have practised it). . . . The Scripture says : They will deride and abuse us, moreover they will lay upon us with sword and rod, etc. In this present world, who was derided and abused and attacked by sword and rod for the Hokekyo's sake, but Nichiren. This prophecy of Buddha is a lie but for Nichiren's realization. Moreover, the Scripture says : We shall be repeatedly driven out, etc. If I, Nichiren, had not been exiled and driven out so many a time, then

what will Buddha do with the word '*repeatedly.*'
Even the Great Masters Tendai and Dengyo could not
read *this word*, how much less others ! Only I, Nichiren,
myself have read it, as being the symbol of the Latter
Law—it is called by Buddha the fearful Evil Days. . . .

" Who shall be able to help Buddha's prophecy, as
the practitioner of the Hokekyo, but for Nichiren ? . . .
I am correspondent to the words of the Scripture. . . .
However, why does not Heaven help me wherein the
world's doubts and my own doubts exist ? I understand that all the Heavens and the guardian deities
have vowed to do their duties in the presence of the
Buddha. Therefore even though he be a monkey who
preaches the Hokekyo, all the deities must respect and
protect him.

" But alas there is no such a protection of me, so how
can I truly be the practitioner of the Hokekyo ? This
doubt is the main point of the present work and the
most important problem of my whole life, therefore
I shall cause the doubt to be greater and I shall reply
to it, in addition to describing it in this essay wherever
the need is felt " (Works, pp. 42–3).

According to " Opening the Eyes," Nichiren deeply
confessed his sins of the past. All the persecutions
must be retributions for his past sins in a sense, he
acknowledged it himself thus ; besides, he confessed
that when he was quite young he was a believer of
Amita Buddha, and he thought at that time that not
even one in a thousand of all the readers of the Hokekyo
could attain Buddhahood, but such a view it is true
originated in his deepest sins which had accumulated
from eternity. But he fortunately awoke to the

Truth of the Hokekyo, and in consequence of its signification he could have typical practices, by which only we can attain the forgiveness of our sins. In that sense his acceptance and submission to persecutions were sufficient to atone for his sins. Therefore he expressed his gratitude to the persecutors. Thus he contended that persecutions do not disannul him from being the practitioner of the Hokekyo. Whoever may take up the martyr's task for the Hokekyo's sake in the days of Evil age, the Latter Law, against all the people, terrible persecutions will surely be heaped upon him, as it is written in the Scripture. Nay, indeed, one who proclaims the Hokekyo in the days of the Latter Law is unable to testify himself as the prophesied man without such persecutions. Persecutions thus are inevitable things to him, the prophesied man. Whatever terrible persecutions might happen, nevertheless one must hold with and proclaim righteousness for righteousness' sake. That is the only way to Buddhahood. He writes in it :

" Let Heavens deprive me of their protection ! Let all troubles crowd upon me ! I will propagate the Law at the risk of my life. . . . Whether for good or for evil to renounce the Hokekyo is to be doomed to go to Hell. I have made a grand vow. I will face threats and temptations of whatever kind they may be. If it were said to me, Thou canst inherit the throne of Japan, if thou wouldst abandon the Hokekyo, and obtain everlasting Happiness according to the doctrine of *the Kangyo* (the Scriptures of the Nenbuts Sect), etc. ; or that thy parents shall be beheaded unless thou callest on the name of Amita-Buddha, etc.

All these troubles shall not affect me, I shall remain unmoved, they will not attract me, except a wise man with his wisdom has it in his power to disprove my principles. All other dangers shall be the dust against a wind. I will be the *Pillar* of Japan, I will be the *Eyes* of Japan and her *Great Ship* will I be. Thus do I make oath, which must not be broken " (Works, p. 75).

Thus he finished " Opening the Eyes " in two volumes, amidst snowy winds in the desert. When spring came he changed his dwelling place by official order for *Ichinosawa*, which is not very distant from the former place. The local chief of that part by degrees showed kindness to Nichiren, and eventually some of his family became his converts.

The following year, 1273, was the most important year to him. He had explained his own personality and mission, so now his systematized philosophy of religion must be the next course to follow. Early in the year, he wrote " The Heritage of Buddha's Introspective Religion " (*Hokkeshū Naishō Buppō Kechimyaku* Works, pp. 294–301), which he clearly laid down as follows :

" The heritage of my religion can adopt Tendai's view of Heritage mainly, but from the true introspective point of view, only the Buddha Shakamuni and Honge Jogyo are the ancestors."

According to this, it is certain that Nichiren's heritage of Buddhism is derived from the Buddha Shakamuni's introspection directly through the medium of the conception of Honge Jogyo's personality. In April, he wrote an essay, " *The Spiritual Introspection of the Supreme Being, Revealed for the First Time in the Fifth Five Hundredth Year after the Tathagata's Death,"* which is the chief work among the important works. His doctrine, the Fivefold Three Divisions were set down in this essay. All aspects of his doctrine and thoughts are strictly united here, so it is said that this essay is indeed the fundamental one concerning Nichirenism. And it must be noted by readers that nobody will understand this essay fully unless he reads the whole works carefully in order to get preparatory knowledge for the essay, and also the Hokekyo as the fundamental article for this single essay. We can read and understand well any other Buddhist articles if we know certain technical terms in general and have an idea of Buddhism, but it must be admitted that this essay needs deeper knowledge than knowledge of Buddhism in general. Therefore when we read it we must include his whole works as its interpretation.

Besides, Nichiren wrote three important essays in succession after this work, they are " Suchness of Being," " The Practice in accordance with Buddha's Instruction " and " The Realization of Buddha's Prophecy." In each of them he firmly expressed his conviction that he was the prophesied man, and at the same time he warned his disciples that come what may, they must not fear death if they will be the right practitioners of the Hokekyo.

He is no longer a mere Japanese priest ; he is rather a personality of great significance for the world at large ; so he says :

" My words (which have been predicted concerning

my conviction of Honge Jogyo) may sound very boastful, but they were intended for the sake of helping the realization of Buddha's prophecy. . . . At any rate, who shall be qualified to be Honge Jogyo other than Nichiren, myself ? The moon rises in the west and shines on the east, the sun rises in the east and shines on the west. Buddhism, too, is just like this. It came from the west to the east during the two thousand years of the Right and Fanciful Laws, but in the days of the Latter Law, Buddhism is to go for the sake of salvation from East to West. . . . According to Buddha's prophecy and considering all circumstances, now, Nichiren's age corresponds with the beginning of the Fifth Five Hundred Period. The True Buddhism shall go to the world from the Far East, Japan " (Works, p. 476).

Thereupon, Nichiren diagrammatized the Supreme Being, in the Circular on the 8th in the 7th month. He wrote in the Circular on the right hand :

" This is the Great Maṇḍala which has never before appeared throughout the world during over the two thousand two hundred and twenty years which have elapsed since Buddha's Death."

On the left hand :

" Having been sentenced (to death) on the twelfth day of the ninth month, in the eighth year of Bunnei, and having been later exiled afar to the Isle of Sado, on the eighth day of the seventh month, in the tenth year of the same, Nichiren drew up this Circular, for the first time."

" Opening the Eyes," " Introspection of the Supreme Being " and representation of the Mandala are the three great tasks which were revealed in the island of Sado during his exile. And now these are quite finished. It is impossible for any other great men to take up these things other than Nichiren, even Nichiren could not reveal these before he was exiled to Sado. He felt the greatest happiness in a religious sense and he was in ecstasy while he was suffering from material needs (Works, p. 478).

Although he was an exiled man, he was always obliged to keep several disciples because, now and again, some of his disciples came to see him from Kamakura or other districts. Of course, Nichiren did not expect to have to keep such visitors, however, according to his description he always had at least seven or eight of these persons. Shijo and others, therefore, always used to send him rice, money and so forth (Works, p. 492). On the one side, Ryokan and men of the same mind had never neglected Nichiren. On the other side, a *Dōkan*, who was one of Ryokan's disciples, and certain others congregated one day and laid their heads together concerning Nichiren, because since he arrived there many people gradually became his converts. Therefore they were greatly panic-stricken for they were professional religionists, and they spoke as follows :

" We shall be dying of hunger as long as we are in such circumstances. We must in some way cause his death. What shall we do now that most of the population of the island have become his converts ? " (Works, pp. 40–43).

Thereupon, Dokan and others came up to Kamakura and stated their views to Nobutoki, one of the authorities of the Hojos. They said :

" As long as Nichiren stays at Sado, we shall not have a single temple nor a priest of our persuasion. Nichiren throws Amita Buddha's images into the fire or into the river. Moreover he used to climb up the hill and pronounce anathemas against the government to the sun and moon with loud voice " (Works, p. 404).

Besides, Ryokan and his fellow-thinkers instigated Nobutoki. Hereupon, he issued forged orders (Works, pp. 494-5) not only on one occasion but three times, that any one becoming Nichiren's convert would be severely punished. Nevertheless all these plots came to naught, and at last the time came for Nichiren to be released.

Meanwhile, Nichiren's prophecy of the internal disturbances and a foreign invasion were gradually realized. These things assuredly caused a panic among the authorities of the government. The Mongolian envoy came in October of the same year of Nichiren's exile to Sado, and in the following year again, and again in the following year. The official authorities gathered together and held a consultation about Nichiren's release. Nearly all the authorities were of one mind with Nobutoki, under the control of Ryokan, so that they determined that Nichiren should never be released. In spite of every man's opposition, the Shikken, the highest authority, namely *Hojo Tokimune* alone claimed Nichiren's release, and in consequence (Works, p. 618) Nichiren was unexpectedly released from the exile of Sado. He received the letter of pardon on the 8th of March, 1274, and the letter was dated the 14th of the second month. The plot of the opponents thus ended in bringing a hornets' nest about their ears. Nichiren left the isle of Sado on the 13th of March. Whereupon they again held a consultation concerning the great enemy of Amita Buddha. They spoke thus :

" It is deeply to be regretted that he has been allowed to return alive even though he is released " (Works, p. 404).

Nichiren left the island as soon as he got the letter of release while they were preparing to attack him in several ways. When he arrived on the main land, he again heard of the opponents' plot against him, namely all kinds of Nichiren's opponents did not like to let him pass alive. They said :

" All the monks of the island are good-for-nothing fellows to have sent Nichiren alive here. But we shall never allow him to pass the front of Amita Buddha's image alive " (Works, p. 404. The place is the famous centre of Amita Buddhism in the provinces of Echigo and Shinano).

Nevertheless, this time, the Government conveyed Nichiren with the official guard so that they could not carry out their plan. Thus Nichiren returned to Kamakura on the 26th of March, over four calender years after he had been exiled.

9. Nine Years on Minobu

Nichiren thus arrived at Kamakura triumphantly and all his followers were extremely joyful. The government seemed to like to listen to Nichiren's view concerning the threatened Mongolian invasion, and he was asked to attend at the office on the 8th of April, ten days after his return. Let us have his own statement :

"They all welcomed me with great courtesy, differing extremely from their former attitude. I was asked questions by some of them concerning Amita Buddhism ; others put questions to me regarding the Shigon Sect ; others again wished to know about the Zen Sect. Hei no Saemon himself asked concerning the efficacy of the doctrine which was taught prior to the Hokekyo. In reply to one and all of them I quoted the Scriptures. Hei no Saemon, on behalf of His Excellency the Shikken, was eager to hear of me whether and when an invasion of the Mongols was expected. I replied, 'In all likelihood before the close of the year. . . . In that connection it was a great pity that you did not listen to my warning which I had already declared to you'" (Works, p. 405; cp. pp. 145–6, 962, 407).

Nichiren renewed his strong remonstrances without yielding this time either. He warned the authorities vigorously about religion and politics, and about the Mongolian invasion. In these eventful days the government was forced to listen to him, and so the government offered him a great sum of fief and asked him to pray for the nation against the Mongolian invasion. Moreover, the government gave him a licence for his propagation. But, of course, Nichiren would not accept such things because they did it for policy's sake, and not out of faith and true understanding. For him, it was impossible to accept anything in a religious sense from those who were not true converts.

At any rate he had done everything which he ought to do, and he had also proclaimed everything which he had to announce. He fought a severe and a long fight throughout his life for righteousness' sake, and now one thing remained, namely to prepare for the future. The signification of the Sacred Title was revealed in the days of Kamakura, and the Supreme Being, too, was established during his exile in Sado. And then, one point among the Three Secret Laws still remained unrevealed. At any rate, Nichiren refused the official proposal. He had already warned and reasoned with the government three times, (Works, pp. 407, 556; cf. p. 909), and yet the government did not obey, although they praised him. Now, the time was at hand for a new movement, so Nichiren firmly made up his mind to retire to some tranquil place in order to undertake the education of his followers and disciples, and also for the sake of something important.

He had decided to retire while he was still in Sado, and he was now only going to perform the preconcerted act. He left Kamakura for good in order to go to Minobu on the 12th of May.

On reflection after due consideration, he selected Minobu for his place or retirement. What is the

signification of his retirement thither? The following
reasons will show us :

1. For the sake of religious service.
2. For the sake of writing essays.
3. For the sake of education.
4. For the sake of preparation of the establishment
   of the Holy Altar.

As he stated, first of all, he wanted to serve his Primeval
master, the Buddha Shakamuni, which he had not
been able to do whole-heartedly, his active life having
so far prevented him owing to his continuous propagation. He was entirely free from any oppression for
the very first time, and he fully appreciated the nature
of tranquillity. From his past experiences, coupled
with his present desire for tranquil religious service,
he always thought over human destiny. The following
old poem was one of his favourite recitations :

> " Through having served the master
> Amassing wood and herbs for him
> And providing him with water,
> Have I acquired this enlightenment of Hokekyo."
>
> (Works, p. 412).

He appreciated the truth of the Hokekyo in living
his simple life in the seclusion of the mountains in
serving his master, the Buddha Shakamuni. He
composed a lyric poem which runs as follows :

> " These floating clouds heaped upon me,
> And obscuring the world and beings,
> Shall be dispersed by truth, the cooling breeze,
> Which is constantly blowing from Vulture Peak."
>
> (Works, p. 417).

Again he writes :

" There is, indeed, no way to attain Buddhahood without having served the Master " (Works, p. 412 ; the work is entitled " Record of Minobu ").

These statements tell of some aspects of the reasons of his retirement. On the other hand, he devoted himself to giving many practical directions of how to live. More than half of his extant works were written in Minobu days. Moreover, he started technical lectures for students in order to educate his followers. But the most important signification consists in his long-cherished desire for preparation of the establishment of the Holy Altar at a certain future. He, indeed, thought of *Mt. Fuji* as the ideal place for the establishment of the Holy Altar of the Honmon Centric Hokekyo. Therefore, he selected this recess of Minobu which is close to Fuji in order to view it and encourage his great ideal. Therefore, he once climbed Fuji and buried rolls of Hokekyo in order to reveal its symbolical signification. The reasons and signification of his retirement to Minobu were un-researched during seven hundred years. According to Tanaka's opinion these were his objects, and this is now the acknowledged view since Tanaka's theory appeared. There actually exist at the present day the remains of the concrete preparation for the establishment of the Holy Altar in the outskirts of Mt. Fuji.

Well, let us grasp how he spent his nine years in the mountains of Minobu. The place where he decided to live for ever was surrounded by lofty mountains on all sides. When he announced his intention of retiring, he received many invitations of welcome from his disciples from various quarters. Nevertheless he politely declined all invitations, and without paying a visit to anybody, even to those who lived near the way which leads to Minobu, thus did he retire into the recesses of Minobu. The following letter will express his heart's sentiments :

" I thought I should retire to some seaside or mountainous resort to my liking, because I was so fearfully persecuted in spite of my benevolent propagation for the sake of true salvation. But, still I thought I would reason with Hei no Saemon once more in order to save the nation which was in danger. After I spoke my words to him, I did not care to stay there any longer, so I left Kamakura, passing by your place. How many thousand times did I think of going to see you all, even against your will, but all the same I passed without calling, struggling within myself."

He thought of his surroundings, for instance the above statement is followed by :

" Because the Province of *Suruga* is the domain of His Excellency Hojo Tokimune, and especially because many court-ladies dwell there. Without doubt, they hate me as an enemy of the Lords of the Saimyoji and Gokurakuji, therefore, if they heard my visit there, you would be molested. So I did not visit you out of kindness, still I am not forgetful. It is the reason I did not send you any reply to your letters until to-day. I am used to giving instructions to those who pass by Fuji and *Kashima* on their way hither or to this part not to call. But I wonder whether they obey my instructions " (Works, pp. 508–9).

Thus he retired, and he resolved never to appear before the public again because he had much to do there ; so he says :

" Whatever command the Emperor or Empress may despatch, I should not discuss Buddhism with any one nor go down from this mountain " (Works, p. 324).

He was welcomed by the lord of the district, *Hakiri*, who was one of his adherents. He built a simple hut in a vale, refusing Lord Hakiri's proposal, but it was destroyed by the wind and snow after some four years. Therefore he had to build a new one. Let him give his account of it.

" There have elapsed some four years since I built a temporary hut of wood on the 17th of July in the eleventh year of Bunnei. Day by day the pillars were corroding and the walls were falling, nevertheless without repairing the hut I read the Scriptures, with the moonlight breaking through the crevices and the draughts turning over the pages one after another so that I had not to turn them over myself. But, alas, in this year, the twelve pillars of the hut fell down in four different directions and the walls also. Every kind of mortal life in short. Let the moon dwell in the hut, let rain pour in, I did not care until now. But now I am repairing the hut with the aid of my disciples, because we cannot have workmen here in the mountains. And from time to time we subsist on snow instead of on food, i.e. when provisions fail us " (Works, p. 987).

Many disciples and followers came and stayed at Nichiren's hut in their longing for their master. Nichiren always welcomed them and used to give them

N

instruction concerning all aspects of life and religion, and he was quite contented with the simple life. He felt quite happy in spite of living in straitened circumstances ; not only that, but he kept a large number of people, from forty to a hundred (Works, pp. 937-8 ; cf. pp. 1331, 725). He received a bag of laver from one of his followers in the Province of Awa, which is Nichiren's beloved native seacoast, in the second month of the year following his retirement. The following lines will express his sentiments :

" Many thanks for the kind presentation of lavers from your good mother and yourself. . . . However, I had nearly forgotten my native village. It was out of my mind, but these lavers awakened in me yearning memories of my boyhood. The lavers are indeed like those I used to see on the seashore of my native province, just the same in colour, appearance and taste. So I cannot help weeping and feeling sad thinking of my parents' death " (Works, pp. 1072-3).

Whenever he felt under an obligation to his followers, he always wrote letters of polite gratitude, combined with praise for their help to him who is living for the sake of the Truth. Without exception, he associated their material help with the consciousness and signification of accumulation of the true virtues. Because he was the practitioner of the Hokekyo and without his existence the Scripture could not be realized. Therefore, to help him means to help the realization of the true Buddhism.

" I received the wheat . . . . I suppose that although you must really be busy, nevertheless you have thought of me and my conditions of life here in the mountains. Thus you uphold the life of the Hokekyo and all the Buddhas in the past, present, and future, like a bird feeding a fledgling or a man pouring oil on a flame, or rain falling on withering grasses or a mother giving the breast to her infant. Your deeds shall open the eyes of all nations ; they are more than words can express '' (Works, p. 965).

Meanwhile, after the lapse of six months since Nichiren warned the government with the words, " In all likelihood before the close of the year " concerning the Mongolian invasion, he wrote in the following strain to one of his converts :

" It seems that the Mongolian invasion is approaching " (Works, p. 813).

Just as he thought, the Mongolian army attacked Japan in a large force in October of the same year. The Mongols captured the Isles of *Tsushima* and *Iki*, and the Mongolian army landed at a part of *Kyūshū*. But most of the Mongolian fleet got shipwrecked in a sudden gale (Works, pp. 503, 496–7). In April of the year following the Mongols sent messengers to Japan. The Hojos government killed them at Tats no Kuchi on the 7th of September and strengthened the defences. In regard to this, Nichiren says :

" It is a great pity that the government beheaded the innocent Mongolian messengers " (Works, p. 1043).

Abuts of Sado developed his understanding and faith ever so much after seeing Nichiren off. He visited Nichiren three times in the Mountains of Minobu from

the remote island of Sado. In spite of his advanced
age, viz. in his eighties, he always used to carry several
kinds of presents to the recesses of the mountain where
Nichiren dwelt. Surely the aged visit of an old grey-
haired man from afar was warmly welcomed by his
master in the quiet mountains. Nichiren used to send
letters to Abuts' wife through the medium of her
husband on his way home. In one of the letters to
her, he says :

" When I was exiled in Sado, you and your good
husband used to send me food at midnight for fear of
being seen. Moreover, sometimes you were wishing to
sacrifice yourselves for me at the risk of your lives
without even fearing the official threats. Therefore
when I left Sado, which was the bitterest place of the
exile, I felt as if my heart were left behind me and I
hesitated to leave. I believed in our affinity for all
eternity. I never dreamt of meeting you or your
husband again in such a place as this spot, but contrary
to my expectations you sent me such a loving husband
as yours from a far away distant shore. I fell into a
dream-like ecstasy. Though I cannot see you, I
always think of your kindness. When you long to see
me, Nichiren, look in reverence at the rising sun or the
moon rising in the evening. I am always reflected in
the sun and moon " (Works, pp. 1054-5).

Abuts paid his last visit to Nichiren when he was
ninety summers old, and he passed away the following
year.

Nichiren wrote the " Selection of the Times " in
1275, and in the next year he wrote " Recompense of
Indebtedness " with reference to his previous old

master Dozen's death.   In it Nichiren proclaimed that the most significant aspect of ethics, namely, the signification of life, consists in the recompense of indebtedness or grace, and he firmly believed that the true orders of human society will be born from it. Nichiren sent his messenger with this essay to his native village in order that he should read it over Dozen's tomb.   He concluded the essay as under :

" Flowers again return to the root and fruits abide on the earth.   Let all these merits be dedicated to the deceased Master Dozen " (Works, p. 197).

Then again, after he left Kamakura and retired from activity his disciples stood in the front rank of the propagation, and consequently persecutions and various obstacles were put in the way of his followers. For instance, the event of Lord *Ikegamis*, or that of Shijo Kingo, or the persecution of *Atswara* and so forth are representative.   Nichiren always had intimate relations with these events, and he used to give his disciples instruction and direction whenever he was concerned with them.   It is very important to study these affairs in detail in order to make clear our idea of Nichiren's character and at the same time one of the aspects of his life.   But, to my regret, they must be omitted in the present work.

As regards his conviction of Honge Jogyo, it attained perfect maturity.   The following are a few of the examples :

" Already the great Bodohisattova out of the earth has appeared, so that the great Law which the Buddha made over to him, summing up the salient points of His Laws shall be in evidence " (Works, p. 325).

" I, Nichiren, am the greatest practitioner of the Hokekyo in the world " (Works, p. 119).

"I, Nichiren am the greatest sage in the world" (Works, p. 513).

Moreover, he wrote clearly identifying himself as the Honge Jogyo in one of the representations of the Supreme Being which he diagrammatized in the mountains of Minobu ; it runs as follows :

" In the beginning of the Fifth Five Hundred Period the Bodohisattova Honge Jogyo appeared and propagated this Law for the first time."

Thus his conviction was, now, expressed perfectly and there is no more doubt that his firm conviction of being the prophesied man in the beginning of the Fifth Five Hundred Period, was firmly realized. He wrote " On the Three Great Secret Laws " in 1281, and in it he tried to make suggestions rather concretely concerning the Holy Altar. In the summer of the same year, the Mongols again attacked Japan. The army claimed to be 150,000 strong. This time, too, fortunately, the Mongolian fleet was destroyed by a gale so that Japan won a great victory perfectly. Nichiren believed himself to be the only authoritative prayer in this national calamity (Works, p. 508), he therefore prayed for Japan's sake, with his special diagrammatizing of the Supreme Being, for the protection of the country. At the same time he sent a special circular to his followers. It says :

" The Great Japan is now being attacked by the Little Mongols. I beseech all my disciples and all those who are on my side to keep quiet and not to argue thereupon among themselves nor with others. Should anybody infringe these instructions he shall be excommunicated. Let this be made public " (Works, p. 621).

With regard to the above quotation, Anesaki explained the point in his work, so let us cite his lines:

" The expression is so terse that it can be taken in more than one way, especially when we remember that Nichiren had always seemed to hail the Mongols as an instrument to awaken the nation. But one thing is clear ; in this letter he used for the first time the phrase, ' the Little Mongols,' the opposite of the usual designation, ' the Great Mongols.' The Mongols, physically great and formidable, were little from the prophets' point of view ; while, as is evident from his previous writings, the actual Japan was for him a degenerate nation, doomed to ruin, but the ideal Japan was great and impregnable " (Anesaki, Nichiren, p. 126).

At any rate, both in human and divine aspects Nichiren was surrounded by many events and troubles which constantly succeeded one another.

10. HIS DEATH

After four years had passed since Nichiren retired to the mountains, he had fallen into weakness and illness. He reported his illness in one of his letters to

Abuts, which was dated the 3rd of July in 1278, he says :

" My age has reached three score, without doubt I feel that I have grown old. Illness and death are what is left. From January of this year to the present, 1st of July, my sickness never left me. By and by, I shall die " (Works, p. 766).

Shijo Kingo was the head physician and Nichiren entirely trusted him, and expressed his thankfulness to the physician over and over again (Works, pp. 811, 935–6, 895, 901, 910). His sickness gradually fell into a critical condition with vicissitudes, and even such a strong sage as Nichiren could not resist its attacks. When he obtained rice and *Sake* (wine) from a lady, one of his followers, he wrote a letter to her wherein he says :

" Since I retired to these mountains I have never been down from them. During these eight years I have been suffering both in body and in mind from illness and age, year after year. Since last Spring, my illness relapsed and especially from autumn to winter my weakness increased day by day, night by night. For these ten days, I have hardly taken any food, and into the bargain the severe cold in the midst of huge snowfalls brought me terrible suffering. My body is cold like a stone, my chest is as cold as ice " (Works, pp. 1020–21).

Nichiren intended to cure his illness at a spa in *Hitachi* Province. He left Minobu, where he had lived for more than eight years, on the eighth of the ninth month. But he was unable to proceed farther, and he stopped at *Ikegami*, near modern Tokyo, where he was welcomed by Lord Ikegami. After arriving at Ikegami, he sent a letter to Lord Hakiri. It was the last letter written by Nichiren. It was dated the nineteenth of the same month and in it he expressed most delicate sentiments. It runs :

" I respectfully beg to state : I have arrived safe and sound at Ikegami. I was extremely happy and deeply grateful to you for having arrived without any troubles, though there were mountains and rivers on my way here, under the protection of attendants who undertook the task by your instructions. Minobu is the place where I shall be back sooner or later, however the expectation might not be realized as I am very ill. Nevertheless, words cannot express my thankfulness for your kindest protection during the past nine years of such a troublesome person as myself and one who lives as I do. Therefore I should like to be buried on the top of Minobu wherever I may die. I became very fond of the chestnut horse which you presented to me, I should like to love him for ever. I want very much to take the horse to the hot water spring of Hitachi but I am afraid he may be stolen there and it would be a great pity if anything should happen to him. Therefore, I think I will ask the Lord of *Mobara* in *Kazusa* to take charge of him until I am back from the spa. Even then I feel uneasy about leaving the horse with a new groom who does not know the horse's ways. Until my return from the spa I want to leave the horse in charge of this groom (who was sent by Lord Hakiri with the horse). Kindly bear this in mind " (Works, p. 629).

Though he was on a sick-bed, he lectured again on his *Rissho Ankoku Ron* for about one month to his disciples and followers, who had flocked to his bedside from east and west. Six elders were appointed as the leaders of his followers on the 8th of October. Nichiren gave his last instruction to them all, and distributed everything to them as mementoes two days later. Moreover he entrusted a boy of fourteen with a great task of propagating the Hokekyo in the Imperial Seat, Kyoto, on the eleventh day. His last moments were approaching. Early in the morning of the 13th day of October in 1282, he was surrounded by his loving followers and disciples, and all of them began to recite the stanzas of Eternity (Kern, p. 307) in the majestic scene which is grandly religious and mournful for men. He calmly clasped his hands and passed away reciting the stanzas with his disciples. He was born a fisherman's son in a small village, and lived as the true practitioner of the Hokekyo and left the world as a sage of the world.

He was cremated on the following day. All his followers left Ikegami with their master's remains on the 21st and arrived at Minobu on the 25th. On the 2nd of December the funeral service was performed. The disciples and followers descended the mountains on the next day and a few elders remained as sextons. On the first anniversary of Nichiren's death the first collection of his works was made. Six elders and other followers undertook the task of propagation and extension. Above all, *Nichiko,* one of the six elders, took steps for the future establishment of the Holy Altar. *Nichiji,* also, one of the six elders, left Japan for Siberia, for the sake of the propagation to the world, soon after the 13th anniversary of Nichiren's death. In concluding this chapter, let us cite one more of his utterances.

" The fact that India was named the Moon-tribe country proves the prophetic truth of the appearance of the Buddha. Our *Fuso* is called Nippon (Japan), the Land where the Sun Rises. Should it not also be the land where the sage is to appear? The moon's course is from West to East, which is a symbol meaning that Buddha's law is East-bound. It is in the East that the sun rises and it is in the West that it sets ; which predicts that Buddha's religion shall return from the land of the rising sun to the land of the Moon-tribe. The moon does not always shine, and in the same manner Buddha only proclaimed the Hokekyo during eight years of his life. The sun is brighter than the moon, and in a similar manner the brightness of the Eastern Sage shall be the light to the dark ages after the Fifth Five Hundred Period " (Works, p. 383 ; cp *ibid.*, p. 476).

V

THE JAPANESE NATIONAL PRINCIPLES

1. The Edict of the Sun-Goddess

NICHIREN sought the ideal country on the earth from his point of view of the Three Secret Laws, especially from the Law of the Holy Altar. It is quite a natural consequence of his doctrine as we have already demonstrated. He found by chance the ideal country in his own native land. Of course, he did not praise Japan on account of its being his Mother Country, but for the sake of her ideal aspects. His several writings will demonstrate it, the writings which previously were translated and cited by the author in the former chapters.

Then, what are the Japanese National Principles which were recognized as the ideal of the world by Nichiren? Well, his problem has a most intimate relation with the theory of the Holy Altar. But the doctrine of the Holy Altar was not so clearly demonstrated until it was fully defined in modern times. As already mentioned, the theory of the Holy Altar was made clear by Tanaka, as also the problems of the Japanese National Principles were explained systematically by Tanaka for the first time at Nichiren's suggestion.

There exist two of the oldest Japanese chronicles, the one is called " *Nippon Shoki* " or " *Nihongi* " and the other " *Kojiki.*"   The former is superior to the latter for several reasons, and is translated into English by Aston, therefore I will explain the former.

Japan was established two thousand and six hundred years ago and has never since been broken nor reformed.   However, there is something that ought to be noted by the nations concerning the history and the ideal of her establishment.

When the Sun-Goddess, the ancestor of the Imperial family and the nation, bestowed the land of Japan on her grandchild, she gave three kinds of treasures, viz. a mirror, a sword and a gem-bead.   And she decided that the Three Treasures should be the signs of the Imperial Throne.   Then what do these three symbolize ?

The Mirror symbolizes Wisdom, the Sword Courage, the Gem-Bead Humanity.   She meant these Three Treasures to interpret the Japanese Imperial Throne. Moreover, the Sun-Goddess commanded by the following edict her August Grandchild, saying :

" This   Reed-plain-1500-autumns-fair-rice-ear Land is the region which my descendants shall be lords of. Do thou, my August Grandchild, proceed downwards and govern it.   Go ! the Imperial Throne shall prosper like unto Heaven on Earth " (this translation is partly Aston's and partly my own.   See " Nihongi " trans. Aston, p. 7, Vol. I.   The Japan Society, London).

By the way, here, the author must give readers a note concerning the above words " shall be lords of " in this translation.   The original was written in Chinese characters and we find it very difficult to translate it into foreign languages. In the above case " shall be lords of " is written in the following manner : 可 王.

The first character was translated into " Shall be " and the second letter corresponds to " lords," King " or " Emperor," etc. But, the first letter in this case not only means " Shall be " but implies the meaning, " Act the Emperor-path." According to Tanaka's theory these characters are interpreted as follows :

" The significance of the words ' shall be lords of ' is paid little attention to in the Shintoic canon. Only the fact that the successive emperors on the throne in the history since the Divine Age have all acted upon the divine words makes the affirmation a thousand times stronger than any theory or axiom. There are ineffaceable facts of history proving that in Japan there had existed the Sovereign Law which men can never disregard. Such has been the foundation of the Right of throne in Japan.

" Let us examine the significance of the ideographic character 王 (which is pronounced Ō and is equivalent to the English monarch, sovereign or King, etc.). There are two meanings of this character. A monarch or a king is 王, while the 王, read according to the free phonetic rule, widens in its sense, in a broader interpretation, the 王 is more than being a simple potentate ; the 王 which means more than a potentate must be exertion of the Rights of Sovereign make perfect the happiness of the people, and that shall be the attainment of the people, and that shall be the attainment of his character. When the Grand Goddess said, ' My descendants shall be lords of ' in the Divine Edict

she verily meant the country to be governed by the 王.
She did not announce to her people, ' See ! there is a
fine country, I endow you with it. Go and rule.'
The divine will was that the country most fitting for
realization of her ideal was discovered, that her
descendants might rule it and that her treasured Right
of Sovereignty might be spread by them for the sake of
humanity. The divine words, ' shall be lords of ' alludes
to all the possibilities and realities of the Imperial
rights and powers " (Tanaka, Japan, the Heaven on
Earth, the 4th Chapter; translation by Kuwabara).

The Three Treasures symbolized the Emperor-Path.
According to the Edict the Sun-Goddess evidently
meant the path, the truth as being the substance of
the Imperial Throne. As far as the Imperial Throne
is concerned with the path of humanity, it shall endure
everlastingly, just as the path is indestructible.
With such a firm conviction the Sun-Goddess announced
that the Japanese Imperial Throne shall prosper as
the Heaven on Earth.

Thus Japan had the Sovereign prior to the establishment of the Empire, and the First Emperor, Jimmu,
founded Nippon (Japan), the Empire of the Rising Sun,
according to the Edict of the Sun-Goddess.

2. THE ESTABLISHMENT OF THE EMPIRE

The Imperial family first dwelt in Kyushu and later
on subjugated *Honshu,* the main land. The *Nihongi*
describes :

" When he (the First Emperor, Jimmu) reached the

age of forty-five, he addressed his elder brothers and his children, saying : ' Of old, our Heavenly Deities *Takami-musubi no Mikoto*, and *Oho-hiru-me-no-Mikoto*, pointing to this land of fair rice-ears of the fertile reed-plain, gave it to our Heavenly ancestor, *Hiko-ho no ninigi no Mikoto*. Thereupon *Hiko-ho no ninigi no Mikoto*, throwing open the barrier of Heaven and clearing a cloud-path, urged on his superhuman course until he came to rest. At this time the world was given over to widespread desolation. It was an age of darkness and disorder. In this gloom, therefore, he fostered justice, and so governed this western border. Our Imperial ancestors and Imperial parent, *like gods, like sages, accumulated happiness and amassed glory*. Many years elapsed. From the date when our Heavenly ancestor descended until now it is over 1,792,470 years. But the remote regions do not yet enjoy the blessings of Imperial rule. Every town has always been allowed to have its lord, and every village its chief, who, each one for himself, makes division of territory and practices mutual aggression and conflict.

" ' Now I have heard from the Ancient of the Sea, that in the East there is a fair land encircled on all sides by blue mountains. Moreover, there is there one who flew down riding in a Heavenly Rock-boat. I think that this land will undoubtedly be suitable for the *extension of the Heavenly task*, so that its glory should fill the universe. It is, doubtless, the centre of the world (see Yamakawa, ' On the centre of the world '). The person who flew down was, I believe, *Nigihaya-hi*. Why should we not proceed thither, and make it the capital ? '

" All the Imperial Princes answered, and said : ' The

truth of this is manifest. This thought is constantly present to our minds also. Let us go thither quickly.' This was the year *Kinoye Tora* (51st) of the Great Year '' (i.e. the Chinese cycle of sixty years ; Aston, Vol. I, pp. 110–11).

On the 5th day of the 10th month of the same year, 667 B.C., the Emperor in person led the Imperial Princes and a naval force on an expedition against the East. He reached the Main land after a few years. Let the Chronicle tell the story :

'' Summer, 4th month, 9th day. The Imperial forces in martial array marched on *Tatsuta*. The road was narrow and precipitous, and the men were unable to march abreast, so they returned and again endeavoured to go eastward, crossing over Mount *Ikoma*. In this way they entered the inner country (*Yamato*). Now when *Naga-sune-hiko* (the native chief under the leadership of *Nigihayahi no Mikoto*) heard this, he said : ' The object of the children of the Heavenly Deity in coming hither is assuredly to rob me of my country.' So he straightway levied all the forces under his dominion, and intercepted them at the Hill of *Kusaka*. A battle was engaged, and *Itsuse no Mikoto* (the elder brother of the Emperor) was hit by a random arrow on the elbow. The Imperial forces were unable to advance against the enemy. The Emperor was vexed, and revolved in his inmost heart a divine plan, saying : ' *I am the descendant of the Sun-Goddess, and if I proceed against the Sun to attack the enemy, I shall act contrary to the way of Heaven.* Better to retreat and make a show of weakness. Then sacrificing to the Gods of Heaven and Earth, and bringing on our backs

o

the might of the Sun-Goddess, let us follow her rays and trample them down. If we do so, the enemy will assuredly be routed of themselves, and *we shall not stain our swords with blood*" (Aston, Vol. I, p. 113).

Many stories are told after this description, but we will omit them and proceed to the end of the story.

"Now *Naga-sune-hiko* sent a foot-messenger, who addressed the Emperor, saying: 'There was formerly a child of the Heavenly Deity, who came down from Heaven to dwell here, riding in a Rock-boat of Heaven. His name was *Kushi-dama Nigi-haya-hi no Mikoto.* He took to wife my younger sister *Mikashiki-ya-hime* of whom he at length had a child, named *Umashi-ma-te no Mikoto.* Therefore did I take *Nigi-haya-hi no Mikoto* for my Lord, and did service to him. Can it be that there are two seeds of the children of the Heavenly Deity? Why should any one else take the name of Child of the Heavenly Deity and therewith rob people of their dominions? I have pondered this in my heart, but have as yet failed utterly to believe it.' The Emperor said: 'There are many other children of the Heavenly Deity. If he whom thou has taken as thy Lord were truly a child of the Heavenly Deity, there would be surely some object which thou couldst show to us by way of proof.' *Naga-sune-hiko* accordingly brought a single Heavenly-feathered-arrow of *Nigi-haya-hi no Mikoto,* and a foot quiver, and exhibited them respectfully to the Emperor. The Emperor examined them, and said: 'These are genuine.' Then in his turn he showed to *Naga-sune hiko* the single Heavenly-feathered-arrow and quiver which he wore. When *Naga-sune-hiko* saw the

Heavenly token he became more and more embarrassed But the murderous weapons were already prepared, and things were in such a state that he was unable to pause in his career. Therefore he adhered to his misguided scheme, and would not alter his purpose.

" *Nigi-haya-hi no Mikoto*, knowing from the first that the Heavenly Diety had simply generously bestowed the Empire on the Heavenly Grandchild, and that in view of the perverse disposition of *Naga-sune* it would be useless to instruct him in the relation of Heaven to Man (i.e. of Lord and Vassal), put him to death. He then came with his army and made submission. The Emperor, who from the first had heard that *Nigi-haya-hi no Mikoto* had come down from Heaven, finding that he now had actually performed faithful service, accordingly praised him, and was gracious to him. He was the ancestor of the *Mono no Be* House " (Aston, Vol. I, pp. 127–8).

Thus the Emperor Jimmu restored peace, and he announced the Ideal of the Establishment of the Empire prior to the proclamation of the accession. The Chronicle states :

" 3rd month, 7th day. The Emperor made an order, saying : ' During the six years that our expedition against the East has lasted, owing to my reliance on the Majesty of Imperial Heaven, the wicked bands have met death. It is true that the frontier lands are still unpurified, and that a remnant of evil is still refractory. But in the region of the Central Land there is no more wind and dust. Truly we should make a vast and spacious capital, and plan it great and strong.

" ' At present things are in a crude and obscure

condition, and the people's minds are unsophisticated. They roost in nests or dwell in caves. Their manners are simply what is customary. *Now if a great man were to establish laws, justice could not fail to flourish. And even if some gain should accrue to the people, in what way would this interfere with the Sage's action?* Moreover it will be well to open up and clear the mountains and forests, and to construct a palace. Then I may reverently assume the Precious Dignity, and so give peace to my good subjects. *Above, I should then respond to the kindness of the Heavenly Powers in granting me the Kingdom, and below, I should extend the mind which will foster Righteousness throughout the line of the Imperial descendants.* Thereafter the capital may be extended so as to embrace all the six cardinal points, and the eight cords may be covered so as to form a roof. Will this not be well ? ' "*

Further on :

" Year Kanoto Tori, first month, first day. The Emperor assumed the Imperial Dignity in the Palace of Kashiwa-bara. This year is reckoned the first year of his reign " (Aston, Vol. I, p. 132. The first year is said to correspond to 660 B.C.).

The above statement is the summary of " the Nihongi " concerning the history of the establishment

---

* From " I should extend " to " the Imperial descendants " is my translation. Aston's translation runs as follows : " I should extend the line of the Imperial descendants and foster rightminded-ness." The points and cords both mean the Universe or the world. " Roof " may also be translated " family," i.e. the Universal family. (Aston, Vol. I, p. 131).

of the Empire. This chronicle was written in Chinese characters and compiled by the official authority about a thousand years after Jimmu's era. Of course, this was written mainly according to a story handed down from the ancient people. But at the same time, as " the chronicle " shows, doubtless this chronicle was written with reference to books extant at that time. The earliest historical work is *Kujiki*, Chronicle of old matters in Ancient times, which was compiled in A.D. 620 under official authority. But it was destroyed by fire in 645. Consequently the " Nihongi " is the only earliest chronicle in Japan. There are many doubts concerning the former volumes of this chronicle from a historical point of view. Many scholars have discussed them. Nevertheless the statement of the chronicle must not be regarded as a mere mythological story. The statement of the Nihongi is indeed the faith of the nation and the principle of the State. Even supposing that it might have been written as a fiction, nothing could interrupt the ideal of the nation. We find its value in the fact that it had the strongest influence on the nation during three thousand years, nay even still at the present day, it is the principle of the nation. Even if it is not matter of fact, at least it is certain that the statement of the chronicle was the national spirit from the ancient ages. At any rate this national ideal during three thousand years was always the supreme reason of the state's existence, no matter what the researches of historians may have been on this particular point.

3. The Three Principles

According to the statement of the Nihongi, which is the national spirit of both the Emperors and the subjects, there are three fundamental principles which are the reason of Japan's existence. The Jimmu's rescript, which was announced prior to his accession ceremony, and the Emperor's proclamation, which was made on his leaving Kyūshu for the main land, will explain the Three Principles.

The Three Principles are, Gathered Happiness, Achieved Glories, and Cultivation of Righteousness. These three are called " Japan's National Principles." But the National Principles are not merely Japan's principles but are indeed meant for the world's benefit. So we must not take a narrow view of the term " the Japanese National Principles " (*Nippon Kokutai* implying : National teaching, fundamental character of the State, the ideal of the country, etc. But it is too difficult to translate formally into any foreign language). The propagation and realization of the Three Principles were believed to be the task of the Japanese nation, of the Emperors and subjects alike. Of course, the Emperors are the masters and the leaders, and the subjects are the assistants. Therefore the Imperial tasks of Japan are called " Heavenly Task " (Tengyo), the term which was used by the Emperor Jimmu. And the Three Principles are the highest rules of Japan, which the Emperors as well as the subjects must obey absolutely and implicitly. The ultimate aim of Japan's Three Principles is absolute peace all over the world. This thought can be seen in the Emperor Jimmu's speech and the successive emperors' words and deeds. The Emperor Jimmu proclaimed :

" We shall not stain our swords with blood."

Further :

" I will now make *ame* (Sweetness) in the eighty platters without using water. If the *ame* is formed, then shall I assuredly without effort and without recourse to the might of arms reduce the Empire to peace."

According to the rules of the Three Principles Japan has kept this ideal of the absolute peace throughout the past. It is not for her own sake but for the sake of all nations. With such conclusive ideals Japan was established, and still exists for this purpose. It is very regrettable that most people of modern Japan have lost sight of their own National Principles. Therefore Nichiren denounced the degenerated Japan while he praised and worshipped the ideal Japan. But Japan has such ideals and principles in her own self, and it is true that Japan is the country of righteousness. But Japan must not boast of the past nor of the present, but of the creation of the future. The signification of the Japanese Throne has thus been realized, as was prophesied by the Ancestor. It was indeed originated in a most religious and moral faith. Let us cite Tanaka's writing about the idea of the Sovereign.

" The soul of the most augustful Divine Edict, the rights of sovereignty have their origin in God's governance of men and men's obedience to God. The sovereign rights are to realize an assimilation of God and Man. God is embodiment of Truth, and when man identifies himself with God he is as one with Truth. This absorption of God and man the ruler of the country strives to bring about. The character 王 signifying monarch or King or sovereign shown in figure, the threefold category harmonized (Works, p. 382), the straight line running perpendicular representing unity. Heaven, Earth and Man, the threefold category, acquire a universal sympathetic life of God's will which is Honesty. The universal phenomena roll on in perfect regularity. The Ruler is careful that he proves himself worthy of the figure 王, and the rights of sovereignty are the schedule of his conduct. He is the Saint of the National Principles."

The term " God " in the above translation is explained by Tanaka as follows :

" Gods and men are not at all unrelated beings. In Christianity, the creator and the created explain the relation between God and man, while in Shintoism and Buddhism God holds different positions in relation to men. The gods as we speak about them here are gods of broader meaning, they being interrelated with representatives of the spiritual world, such as Bodohisattovas, saints, Tathagatas. They are none else but men who had been emancipated, had become enlighteners of their fellow-beings. Gods and men explained thus are essentially an absorption and kindreds. But their respective powers are different. When men work with higher aims their lives become lives of Gods " (Tanaka, Japan, the Heaven on Earth, the fifth chapter. See Tanaka's " The Study of the Japanese National Principles," pp. 32–45).

Further, again, let us cite Tanaka's lines :

" After many struggles he (the First Emperor Jimmu) pacified the middle island, and founded the throne in *Kashiwabara*, Province *Yamato*. In the famous proclamation which he uttered on this occasion, he made it clear that the founding of the Imperial throne was not his personal affair, but it was the realization of the Goddess' truth of humanity, the actuality and harmony of God and Man. The rights of his ancestors were remembered with the words of Gathered Happiness and Achieved Glories, and were taught to be powers of the righteous. The Holiness (which grows of Gathered Happiness) and Valor (which brings about Achieved Glories) were qualities of Jimmu's ancestors, deities whose lives and works the Emperor realized and identified. The Three Principles of Gathered Happiness and Achieved Glories and Cultivation of Righteousness originate in the ancient spirit of Japan. It is the greatest power, originating as it did in Jimmu's Proclamation, which gave birth to the Empire of Japan. . . . The Grand Goddess having favoured her descendants with her achievements, and Jimmu having uttered the commencement of the propaganda of Truth, the works of the righteous have become consummation of Morality, Reason, Truth and Finality. Righteousness is soul of the National Principles. . . . The word ' Righteousness ' is in itself power of truth, and factualizes the redemption of mankind. Happiness spreading above and below, the world reaching final glory, all were brothers of the same family in his mind."

Thus the Japanese National Principles mean indeed

the ideal of mankind, not only that Japan is the typical realization of such ideals. The reason of Nichiren's worship of Japan consists in this respect in spite of his severe attack and criticism of degenerated Japan.

Tanaka's interpretation runs as follows :

" The essences of the National Principles (*Kokutai*) are Entity, Body and Soul. Entity here is to be understood to be appertaining more to Soul than to Body, and the Soul of the country is the same in origin with the fundamental Principles of the country. The Soul of Japan explains the reason for the creation of Japan, the reason of her being. The Heavenly Law ever symphonious and all consistent, has been favourable for her birth and existence and the development of the Higher Morality. This is the fundamental spirit of the National Principles, Japan's Ancient Path. The exegesists have taught that ' Entity is identical with system, and System is Law.' The Principles of the Nation are Entity, and Entity is at once the soul and the character of the nation " (Tanaka, Japan, the Heaven on Earth, the first chapter).

The following quotation was originally written in French by Dr. Paul Richard, of France. It shows how Japan impressed him in a spiritual sense.

To Japan

" I am seeking throughout the world for a just nation, a nation of the future. For the future belongs to the just nations. They shall inherit the earth.

"And lo, many nations make use of the name of Justice. They say : ' We are fighting for Right.' I looked at their hands : they were stained with blood, the blood of their rapines and cruelties. And I turned away. Their path leads down to the night. They are the nations of the past.

" But the nation of the future, the upright nation who, in this conflict unloosed everywhere for the reciprocal judgment of the peoples, would be truly the nation of Right, I am seeking for her throughout the world. That free nation who would fight not to conquer but to liberate, to set free the oppressed peoples, the enslaved races; that strong nation, ally of the weak, who with unstained hand, as the archangel of Justice, would brandish her sword, not to besmear it with blood, but to radiate its light, that just nation where is she? . . .

" I look toward Japan.

" I have come from where the sun is setting; I have come from the West in flames and its empires in ruin, toward thy dawn, Empire of the Rising Sun ! Hark : I will speak to thee as I would speak to my own mother-country. For one day every noble man in Humanity will look upon each nation as his own, will act in each nation as he would towards his own. And I can speak to thee as I could to none other, for thou feelest more deeply. . . .

" Hark and understand. Understand thy destiny as nation in this world ; thy destiny and thy Mission. . . . Thus, during three thousand years thou wert able to form and grow according to thine own law, by favour of a protection which gives thee to-day the unequalled pride, the privilege unique in history, of never having been subjected or vanquished. During three thousand years thou hadst no masters save those whom thy love freely chose, since time immemorial, as the living symbol of divine power. What other nation shares with thee this exceptional fortune of having known throughout the centuries but one line of emperors, one Emperor. For in the eyes of the spirit, is it not always the same who reigns, and can he not, while looking in the sacred mirror of the ancestors, recognize in his own image the image of all those who survive in him ?

" Nation of Asia who alone hast remained free, nation of the earth who alone hast always been so, understand then that thou art born to be a liberator of nations. These are not thine only privileges. Protected against all, none approached thee if not to bring thee something. Thou hast received gifts from all. Each civilization in its turn leaned over thee, as a benevolent fairy, to offer thee her boons. The remembrance of each of them recalls a stage of thy progress. China, and India, and afterwards Europe came towards thee, hands laden with the best they had. And when one day thine enemies themselves faced thee, it was to give thee occasion of becoming greater still.

" Nation of the world who alone has received but benefits from the others, understand that thou art born to be the benefactor of the earth. Thus, the treasures of all accumulated to enrich thee. To the old wisdom were added the sciences, to the heritage of the great past the promise of futures greater still. Placed at the confluence of all the large streams where humanity came to drink, thou hast mingled in thee their contrary currents, thou hast wedded two opposite geniuses, two worlds : Child of the East, heir of its Spiritual riches, thou becomest also child of the West and wert endowed with its Material power.

" First of all the nation in whom the divorced tendencies of the spirit join again, and, as yet, the only one who knows how to unite the thought of Europe and that of Asia, thou art born to become the unifier of those two complementary halves of the future world ; thou art the first nation of that future.

" Land loved by the Gods, they too are reconciled in thee. While everywhere their religions interchange maledictions, thy benevolent cults instead of excluding complete each other : one being that of the divine immanence, of the One in all, in space where move the living forces of nature, in time where dwell the ancestors, living too; and the other that of the transcendence, of all one, beyond time and space, in the eternal repose of the supreme benediction. And are not these two cults also the only ones in this world which have remained clear of bloodshed, the only ones which have preserved the right to say : ' Peace on earth ? '

" Around them, in the shelter of their benevolence, other religions may come to raise their altars, to be pacified, perhaps purified at this contact. And as thou hast received in the past the religion of the Orient, thou receivest to-day that of the Occident, that in which all the Occident mingles, in which the echo of a voice of love rings through the clamours of Judea, of Greece, of Rome and of the New World . . . one teaching that man must become God, and the other that God can become man. But was it not necessary that all, meeting thus, should learn to form together, in unity, the more perfect religion of the future. For the day is coming when, to worship the divine Infinite, man will not find too many all the gods and all their cults. . . . As it is in thee that they assemble, so is it from thee that they await their possible synthesis of harmony, their festival of light, O Child of the Sun !

" Nation whose shores are open toward all shores, making them less distant ; nation whose thought is turned toward all thoughts, reconciling them ; Nation in whom the world seems to seek the scattered rays of its soul, thou art born out of a hope of Humanity ; thou art born as a hope for the birth of Humanity ! . . .

" Coming in a direct line from a past so distant that none have kept the memory of it, thou standest on the threshold of a Future that none can know, but which something in the depths of thyself contemplates. Be not proud of the past, neither of the present, but of the Future. For if others succumb under a too heavy weight of past glories, thine own true glory comes from the Future. Manifest before the nations this glory of the Future. . . .

" People ready for the fight, this master is a divine warrior. Let thy war be worthy of the god who is in thee ! For thou shalt fight. Against whom ? It matters not, so long as thou knowest why. . . . It is a deep reason which wants thee to know first not the enemy thou hast to fight, but the cause thou hast to serve. The enemy of this cause will be thine. Thus of himself he will be revealed. But shouldst thou attempt to discern him otherwise, thou wouldst be misled. . . .

" I heard, amidst the clamour of this world, two voices calling to thee. Discriminate between them and choose. One says, ' Profit. Thy horizon should not exceed the things thy foot encounters, or those thy hands can seize. Remain near them who are strong.

Fear them. And serve them, if needed. . . .' But the other voice says, ' Serve no one. Serve thy mission. Fear no one; fear but one thing: to fail thy mission. Seek no support in the strength of those who seem strong. The past sweeps it away, and thou wouldst go down with it. But be a support for the weakness of those who seem weak. For they are the elect of the beginning Reign. Look forward. Accept not the gains which would cause thy loss. And profit of the hour which is given thee. . . .'

" This voice is the voice of the Lord of thy work. He will accomplish this work with thee, but he can also accomplish it without thee, against thee. To the Lord of the Nations who to-day tills the earth to found there the Kingdom of his Justice, what nation could long offer resistance ? He advances amidst the peoples, and his Judgement precedes him. Vanquished already are those who resist him ; victors from now are those who fight with him. For there is no victor other than himself. And none are vanquished save by him. Thou, beloved people whom he calls, what wilt thou be?

" I saw, I saw thy soul. It was prostrated in silence before him, to receive from him the command, and the promise, the sword of Victories, and the crown of the Future " (pp. 19–35, translated by Mme Mirra Richard, January, 1917).

Doubtless, Mirra Richard's insight, in spite of her being a foreigner, is much deeper than any ordinary Japanese's recognition of the Japanese National Principles.

Well, the first principle is the " Cultivation of Righteousness " which is the highest principle of Japan.

In the original, this cultivation of Righteousness consists of two words, namely " *Yō Sei*." " *Yō* " means cultivation, fosterage, or protection, and " *Sei* " means Righteousness. Now, what is Righteousness ? But, we cannot find the definition of the Righteousness in the First Emperor's own words except in those taught, which were manifested by the Three Treasures.

On the other hand, Nichiren too proclaimed Righteousness, and, as I have mentioned already, he wrote an essay which is entitled Rissho Ankoku Ron, the Establishment of Righteousness. According to Nichiren, the Righteousness can be explained by Nichiren himself from the point of view of the Hokekyo.

Nichiren's proclamation on the establishment of the Holy Altar at a certain future time by unity of true Buddhism and the national law is one of those explanations which I translated and cited in the chapter on the Holy Altar.

The second principle is " Achieved Glories " which resulted from the virtue and effects of Cultivation of Righteousness. Whatever one declares righteousness to be, if this righteousness awakes in the morning and disappears in the evening, then what is the effect ? Even if it is called righteousness, nonetheless such inanimate righteousness shall not be taken account of. On the contrary, since the proclamation of Cultivation of Righteousness was made there have elapsed three thousand years and time is still for ever flying. " If the fountain-head is far away the stream must be proportionately long " (Works, p. 196). The third principle is " Gathered Happiness." Happiness means here benevolence and love with happiness.

These three principles were kept throughout the

Eternal direct Line of the Throne as the Japanese National Principles. Hereupon Nichiren proclaimed that Japan is the ideal country where the Holy Altar of the Hokekyo shall be established. Of course his thought concerning this point cannot be regarded as a mere patriotic biased view. He is, doubtless, the founder of the universal religion, as we have learned already, consequently, on the one hand he rose above the country, while on the other hand he recognized the country as the authoritative organ of the realization of religion and ethics. Therefore Nichiren made the following proclamation concerning the national danger which was caused by the Mongolian invasion :

" We must congratulate ourselves that the Disparagements of the Truth shall diminish even though the State of Japan be destroyed " (Works, p. 813).

Moreover, from the same point of view, he sometimes boldly declared that even the Sun-Goddess is nothing more than a little deity. For Nichiren, therefore, there is nothing but the universal Kingdom of truth, heaven on earth. But, as I have mentioned already, the country must first of all be religionized in order to establish the universal Kingdom of Heaven. From this point of view Nichiren found the ideal country in the very country of Japan, which was established without any doubt on the Righteousness. In this sense Nichiren identified his religion, which is based on the Hokekyo, with Japan's substance. People to-day seem to think Nichiren to have been simply the founder of a sect, but this is quite an error ; because Nichiren declared that he claimed to be neither the founder of any sect nor the successor of any sect (Works, p. 534).

P

But, on the contrary, he exclaimed, " I will be the Eyes of Japan, I will be the pillar of Japan, I will be the great Ship (redemption) of Japan " ; Japan which was regarded as the land of righteousness. To him, in this sense, nothing was of real significance except the realm of Japan, because the world, the morality, the humanity, the Buddha, the God or the truth, all things of life and being would start anew from the Reality of Japan. Thus, Japan as Truth of the world, Japan as the Foundation of Human salvation and Japan as Finality of the world concerning her moral essence and aspects is Japan in her reality. In that connection Nichiren looked upon himself as the leader of the nation and the world ; so he says :

" The future of Japan depends on Nichiren alone . . . Nichiren is the Soul of Japan " (Works, p. 402 ; Nichiren's view on Japan can be seen in the following pages : Works, pp. 2, 68–79, 104, 117, 136, 139, 140, 175–6, 182, 209, 264, 279, 328, 332, 382, 383, 426, 428, 447, 509, 519, 522, 526, 545, 548, 562, 575–6, 593, 604, 615, 759, 789, 790, 905, 930, 976, 1043, 1070, 1110–12, 1328, 1331, 1383, 1453, etc. etc.).

Thus there is no " Only for Japan," but " Japan for Mankind." The Truth of Japan is the Truth of Humanity. The millennium of the world is to be the millennium of Japan. The substance of Japan's primitive national foundations are powers of Achieved Glories and benevolences, of Gathered Happiness, that have grown into the power of righteousness, and the power of righteousness had become the foundation of the Empire and the soul of the nation. Thus the Holy work had begun with the Edict of the Sun-Goddess and the proclamation of the Great Jimmu, and the essential meanings of the National Principles are thus interpreted by Nichiren and Modern Nichirenism.

4. THE GREAT EMPEROR MEIJI

However, Japan was unknown to the world, except in a few cases, during the three thousand years since the Three Principles were announced to the world. About half a century ago Japan appeared before the world during the reign of the late Emperor Meiji the Great. This appearance of Japan before the world's recognition was indeed the first step of the realization of her great ideals.

But the nation is still intoxicated with rich cultivation which was introduced by the Western nations while the nation forgot the ideals of the Mother-country. Of course the present time may be the transition period, nevertheless it is a great pity that the nation's actions are very imitative of European manners while the National Principles are lost sight of. Alone the Great Emperor Meiji always instructed with rescripts or poems throughout his busy life. The Emperor was indeed the incarnation of the National Principles.

He strictly kept the National Principles in His mind and put them into practice. According to the Imperial Ancestor's instruction and to the National Principles, He ruled the State, and his aim was the establishment of the highest humanity in the world. His establishment of the Constitution and the promulgation of the Edicts are witness to his glorious achievement. If any one looks on the Constitution of Japan as a mere foreign imitation he makes a great mistake. The Emperor declared :

" We, ever faithful to the Principles of Our Ancestors and the Imperial propaganda, build up the remainder of their works according to the need of the time."

The words of the Emperor explain the case. The following verses show us how earnestly he strove for the absolute peace of the world :

> " How strange world's waves
> So fiercely do rage
> For to me Humanities
> Are but one family."

And again, the following rescript of the Great Emperor Meiji is the full explanation of Japanese National Principles, which were once called the Heavenly Task by the Great Emperor Jimmu, the founder of the Empire. In the translation by the Department of Education, it says :

" Know ye, Our subjects :

" Our Imperial Ancestors have founded Our Empire on a basis broad and everlasting, and have deeply and firmly implanted virtue ; Our subjects ever united in loyalty and filial piety have from generation to generation illustrated the beauty thereof. This is the glory of the fundamental character of Our Empire (Kokutai ; according to my translation, " the Japanese National Principles "), and herein also lies the source of Our education. Ye, Our subjects, be filial to your parents, affectionate to your brothers and sisters ; as husbands and wives be harmonious, as

friends true ; bear yourselves in modesty and modera-
tion ; extend your benevolence to all ; pursue learning
and cultivate art, and thereby develop intellectual
faculties and perfect moral powers ; furthermore
advance public good and promote common interests ;
always respect the Constitution and observe the laws ;
should emergency arise, offer yourselves courageously
to the State ; and *thus* guard and maintain the
prosperity of Our Imperial Throne coeval with heaven
and earth. So shall ye not only be Our good and
faithful subjects, but render illustrious the best traditions of your forefathers.

" The Way here set forth is indeed the teaching
bequeathed by Our Imperial Ancestors, to be observed
alike by Their Descendants and the subjects, infallible
for all ages and true in all places. It is Our wish to
lay it to heart in all reverence, in common with you,
Our subjects, that we may thus all attain to the same
virtue.

" The 30th day of the 10th month of the 23rd year of
Meiji. (Imperial Sign Manual. Imperial Seal.) "

Dutifulness to parents, trustfulness to brothers and
sisters, love between couples, trust of friendship, the
household virtues, symphonious knowledge, culture,
philanthropy, integrity, chivalry, all these national,
social, family principles are to conform to the Imperial
propaganda of the world's final happiness. The word
thus (or it can be translated *thereby*) means relative
to affinity and sincerity and all other moral qualities as
set out above. Again, in the closing paragraph of the
rescript, the Emperor made it known that Higher
Morality was the transmission of the Imperial ancestors

and primitive duties and ancient faith of the people. This teaching generated from His deepest understanding of the National Principles. According to this teaching, the Japanese as a nation must protect and adhere to the Heavenly task in every aspect with their very lives. Individual morality, morality of the family, social morality, the national morality; education, industry, politics, love, reward for indebtedness and so forth, all of them are mentioned as helping the Heavenly task. This synthetic creation is indeed the Heavenly task for the world's sake. The Great Emperor Meiji also composed innumerable verses, no fewer than 100,000, in which He always used to give instruction to the people. We can grasp His understanding of the National Principles of Japan in these verses. The following are a few examples of His poems:

> Whene'er I open and peruse
>   The chronicles of old,
> I ask, " How fares it with the land
>   Whereof the rein I hold ? "
>
> I gaze oft on the straw-thatch'd hut
>   That hides the lowly swain,
> And wonder how the tenant fares
>   When rage the wind and rain.
>
> From the laws of the Age of Gods*
>   Never may I depart !
> This is the great and main desire
>   That ever fills my heart.
>
> E'en while ye smite with all your might
>   Your country's bitter foe,
> Let not your hearts forget with love
>   Of all mankind to glow !

* i.e. the Imperial ancestors.

As o'er the cheering fire I list
  To wintry blast and shower,
I think oft on the cottager
  In his old draughty bower.

In the excess of fondling love
  That prideful notions breeds,
Let not thy fav'rite garden pets
  Run wild and turn to weeds !

Together with the million souls
  To share the joy of weal
Is of all joys the sweetest far
  That mortal man can feel.

Of sultry summer's swelt'ring heat
  Can I not well complain,
When in the seething slime he stands,
  The patient husbandman !

What easy seems, yet of a truth
  Is oft the hardest strife,
Is well to tread the narrow path
  That leads thee through this life.

When brightly smiles the blue o'erhead,
  Or darkly lowers the sky,
The thought will never leave my mind—
  How feed my flock this day ?

As broad and clear and cloudless as
  The lucid, azure sky
Would I could make my mind and heart,
  With even heaven to vie !

See every shrub and herb its lot
  Of fruit or flower pay !
Naught in the world exists in vain,
  But has its part to play.

It flows and yields, and bends and bows,
   To cup, or sea or brook ;
And yet the drops of water oft
   Will pierce the hardest rock.

As bright and clear and rosy as
   The rising morning sun,
With such a mind and heart and soul
   May everything be done !

When dust amass'd a mountain makes,
   'Tis hard to shake it off ;
So fares it with the man who will
   At trifles laugh and scoff.

Among the mountains I will seek,
   And in remotest isles,
For men of worth unknown to fame,
   On whom no fortune smiles.

What though, with plate and down, thou dost
   In warm affluence bathe,
Let not thy wealth allow thy heart
   To swerve from duty's path !

Far may my mind range o'er the land,
   Throughout its length and breadth,
E'en as the moon above me shines
   On all the world beneath !

Although the rider be as apt
   And skilful as he may,
Let him beware ! No steed but will
   Stumble once in a way.

Inquire we into what befell
   In hoar antiquity,
And render clear the mazy doubts
   That puzzle me to-day !

Never be wroth with Providence
   Nor blame thy fellow men,
But well reflect on thine own fault
   Committed 'yond thy ken !

If fault there be, correct this me
   For that, ye heavenly powers !
The people are my children born
   In good or evil hours.

The dew of mercy falls like rain
   On wicked and on good,
And there is jubilee on earth
   Among the multitude !

The brighest gem, while in the rough,
   Thou thinkest dim and dull,
If thou forget to cut with care
   And polish to the full.

If 'mong the rank and wilding growth
   I choose with heedful mind,
Who knows but I may chance upon
   Some salve to bless mankind ?

Comfort the man who gave thee birth,
   Make glad his aged heart,
When to the land that gave thee birth
   Done is thy daily part.

The bad I'll leave ; the good I'll take
   For the folk in my hands ;
Would I could lift and raise this realm
   Above all other lands !

Select the path of life whereby
   To get on in the world,
My son, and thou shalt come to see
   Aloft some sign unfurl'd.

Let each man play his lotted part
  With punctuality,
And he shall stand with joyful heart
  Beneath the blossoming tree.

'Twixt realm and realm reigns peace again,
  And universal joy ;
I bless my star, that I have lived
  To see this joyous day !

To e'en the loftiest mountain heights
  That tower to the sky
There winds a path meand'ring round
  If thou wilt only try.

Look at the writing of the child
  Striving with ink and pen,
And learn anew the homely truth
  That effort pays all men !

The people's minds are apt to stir
  With every windy gust ;
How shall I clear the murky air
  From blinding, madd'ning dust ?

How prone they are to stray afar
  To where the cliffs sink steep !
'Tis hard to inculcate on men
  How duty's path to keep.

To see the steed, my mate of years,
  Grow aged and infirm
Makes sad my heart, much as to view
  A once straight, now bent form.

These translations are adopted from " A Voice out of the
Serene," by H. Saito.

5. THE NATIONAL SYSTEM

Usually, the science of state embraces dominion, subjects and sovereignty as the three component elements of state. But exception must be allowed to Japan's National system, for Japan, at all events, consists of the following five elements (Tanaka, " The Study of the Japanese National Principles," pp. 30–1) :

1. God (The Sun-Goddess, etc., the ancestors).
2. National Principles (The reason of the establishment).
3. Dominion (The background where the principles are acted).
4. Subjects (The people who realize and practice the Principles).
5. Emperor (The possessor of the dominion, the leader of the nation, the representative of the God).

These five elements, however, are united into the Heavenly task, the National Principles. Therefore, the National Principles are the highest authority of Japan, to which everything must be subjected. Thus Japan which was established by the highest morality, is entrusted with a great mission.

In Japan, the essential cultivation which comes from the National Principles is called " Loyalty and Filial Piety." Of course this Loyalty and Filial Piety is not an abstract theory but the path that ought to be practised. Japanese morality unites every moral aspect into this Loyalty. The conception of Loyalty and Filial Piety is totally different from that of any other country. We mean thereby the embodiment of our lives, so that it does not mean loyalty in the usual sense, which rises from an ordinary indebtedness in a reciprocal sense. It comes only from the absolute faith which is morally refined as applied to life. Therefore, loyalty is not loyalty just because of indebtedness. Loyalty and dutifulness are duties *a priori* of the nation. The Japanese nation grew out of the spirits of loyalty and dutifulness, and the honour and glory of the National Principles will be perpetual with the propagation of loyalty and dutifulness, identified with the words of the Meiji rescript, transmitted with the Ancestors of the Path, which are achievement and consummation. And thus Sovereign and people have worked in mutual support for the extension of the ancient truth and prerogative, and their works concentrated in the Right of the National Principles.

The principle that rules the sovereign and the principle that rules his subjects are different, but the rewards are one and all, because they sprang from the propagation and the realization of the Heavenly task, according to the fundamental National Principles, from the bosom of truth, growing and strengthening with it perpetually. So Nichiren said :

" It is Loyalty and Filial Piety that are necessary for the security and salvation of the world and one's country " (Works, p. 448).

It is impossible to realize a moral world unless we act impartially regardless of all private feelings, especially in an emergency. " To a high sense of duty even a parent must be sacrificed " is the final step in associated human lives. How much more so is the conception of the Loyalty of Japan, which is the most pious faith in the incarnation and leadership of the National Principles. So that this loyalty is the absolute faith in the highest sense in Japan ; Nichiren says :

" If the father betrays the Emperor, the son shall remonstrate with the father on his disloyalty ; and if the father does not follow his advice, the son shall fulfil his duty in the highest sense even if the father is to be sacrificed. This is the greatest filial piety to the father " (Works, p. 58).

Of course, these are ultimate measures where there is force majeure ; and so, all aspects of morality in the usual sense are quite compatible with this highest sense of duty if they are united into the National Principles. Loyalty and filial piety can be distinguished from the point of view of individual existence, that is loyalty for the sovereign and filial duty for parents. But this relation is a relative one, so that in emergencies, both loyalty and filial piety must be dedicated to the Sovereign. The Emperor *Yūryaku* says :

" We are the Sovereign and subjects in the highest sense, but we are the father and sons in as far as our private sentiments are concerned."

The Imperial family is the leader of the nation as well as the father, because the family is the head family of the nation and at the same time the Imperial family has the three virtues, viz. the Leader, the Father and the Sovereign. Thus the nation is understood. Consequently " Loyalty and Filial Piety composes the absolute morality which cannot be compared with any other conception of morality on the same basis.

This relation is the Japanese National system through eternity both with the Emperors and subjects.

Nevertheless Japan welcomes any foreign civilization in order to cultivate herself more and more. Buddhism, Confucianism, Taoism, Christianity and the modern European civilization ; all have been fully introduced. But, let it be said, Japan always Japanizes all civilization introduced into her realm. Accordingly, it would appear as if she had no civilization of her own but only imitated civilization. But if there is any civilization in Japan which is worthy to show to the world, the National Principles are the One. Without any doubt Japan could assimilate perfectly any foreign civilization owing to her own fundamental civilization, the National Principles.

Japan has come into existence with the Heavenly Task, and it has not been imposed upon her to create a civilization of her own. Her work is to adopt the civilizations of the world and make assimilation and revival, that is to say, the synthetic creation. The civilizations of the different nations are judged with a transcendent vision, and recreated into her entire production. The civilization of Corea, of China, of India, and of Europe had come to Japan to undergo her characteristic remodelling, and still it grows and holds sway maintaining their respective original features.

Japan must now express her appreciation to the world at large for their kindness by offering in return her own civilization. But, how regrettable it is that Japan, in a sense, has lost the National Principles out of her mind, that is to say the present Japan is affected with a serious malady. Some day in the near future Japan shall proclaim without hesitation the National

Principles for the sake of the world, and will lay them before the International Conference.

I have stated thus briefly the Japanese National Principles according to Nichiren's doctrine and ideas, and according to the interpretation of modern Nichirenism. The following quotation was proclaimed by Tanaka, which will demonstrate the attitude of Nichirenians.

DECLARATION

(Concerning the Publication of " The Study of the Japanese National Principles ")

On a fortunate day of dedication of a shrine to the Great Emperor Meiji, I declare to make public " The Study of the Japanese National Principles" which is the production of my thinking and researches during these forty years. Ah ! the time has come ! All ye nations ! Study the Japanese National Principles.

Without doubt, the Japanese National Principles are the moral path. The path means the practice of truth. We call it Truth in theory, and Righteousness in a practical path. " Cultivation of Righteousness " is this. The path unites all goodness, hence " Gathered Happiness," and the path implies wisdom, that is to say " Achieved Glories." These are the justice of the universe which all human beings shall trust ; Japan alone is the pioneer to transmit it to posterity, having championed it as the representative of the world. Therefore, although it is called the Japanese National Principles, the path is the path of the world.

Essentially man is the vessel which contains the moral path and not the vessel of nutriment. Therefore, to comprehend man from the point of view of food is

as erroneous a view as to look upon a man as a beast.
All the horrible, combative and bloody happenings
from which the world has suffered throughout history
are but the reflex of an erroneous idea whereby the
moral path was supplanted by food, making a beast
of a man. Must we be scared by errors of thought ?
Surely human beings have now become tired of strife
after the evil consequences of Wars. " How then to
live right " and " how to dwell in safety " are henceforth the problems to solve. The path which abandons
food is the only key. Food can be found in the moral
path but not the moral path in food. If we give up
the path, food will die, if we abandon food, the path
will prosper and food will co-exist. There will no longer
be strife, if the material and the spiritual are united
within internal life, and then peace will exist when
everything is in order externally. This path has been
awaiting man from eternity. The Ancestor, the Sun-
Goddess handed down this Law and proclaimed, " It
shall prosper like unto Heaven on Earth," and the
founder of the Empire, the Great Emperor Jimmu,
succeeded to the Law and declared, " The Eight cords
shall be covered so as to form a roof." How great the
divine task ! There have elapsed 2600 years since
these announcements were made on the earth. The
practice of the moral law is shown in the form of
" Sovereign and Subjects." The thing which is the
highest standard of human cultivation, through sentiment and reason realizing perfect morality, is the form
of the " Sovereign and Subjects " of Japan. The
Heavenly Task " like gods," " like sages," and the
brilliant characteristics of " Emperors of one and the
same Dynasty throughout the ages " and of " The

whole nation of one mind " produced the unique
civilization and the nature of " Loyalty and Filial
Piety " owing to " Wide and profound merit and deep
virtue." In substance, the emperors and subjects are
one body and equal; in efficacy, orders of society,
between the two are distinguished by the observance
of dignity. This mysterious order coincides with true
equality. Such a civilization is tranquil and brilliant.
Therefore in Japan there exists rank but no class-
antagonism. Some there may be who will make rank
the cause for strife, but the cause of this strife is food
and not rank. The rank which was submitted to the
world by Japan at an early age is the form which is
armed with truth for the purification of human beings,
and for the sake of the protection and assurance of the
true value of equality. True equality consists verily
in equitable rank. Probably the solution of human
life culminates here.

The defect of modern civilization lies in ignorance
concerning the origin and end of the material and
spiritual, and in reversing the order of morality and
food. Surely, the collision of material and spiritual
produces destruction and degeneration while the unity
of them brings about a settlement and an exaltation.
The Keeping of a perfect union of the material and
spiritual, the path of " Sovereign and Subjects " which
is the outcome of the Japanese National Principles,
alone can endow mankind with eternal life. Methinks,
this is the new and unique lesson for the modern world
which is gradually awakening from the deepest dream
of intricacy and wildness. Ah ! the time has come !
All ye nations, make a study of the Japanese National
Principles.

Q

VI

CONCLUSION

1. Nichiren's Views on Conduct

Briefly have I stated and pointed out the system, characteristics and problems of Nichiren's religion and thought in the above several chapters. Now, let us add a few words in conclusion concerning its real aspects with reference to modern Nichirenism.

Nichirenism as the practical religion teaches us that human life finds its signification and light by strong procedure and by following the path which leads to promise of life, and which is different from a mere abstract conception of truth. Therefore, for Nichirenians, there is no racial discrimination, nor wrong notion of nationality, nor class, but only one discrimination, viz. between men who obey and safeguard the path and those who do not. It is the universal religion, which is above the usual national conservatism. Nichirenians find their gratitude in their awakening of the path, and, according to Nichiren's definite instruction, they are to share their happiness with all mankind. They will never realize the objective state of faith in individual ease or consolation. They will surely proceed to the movement of reconstruction of the world even if they sacrifice their individual consolation or ease ; but in the very process of that task they will discover the real means of Attainment of Buddhahood. Their expectation will indeed consist in Universal Buddhafication.

Accordingly, Nichiren's faith does not lie within a mere religious sentiment nor in bliss of the Almighty. Their faith only traces their right path wherein their lives consist, therefore God's love is apart from the problem as far as they are concerned with the Heavenly Task. Because protection of righteousness is God's duty.

Of course they do not seek religion in a mere ritual form, though without doubt it is an important part of religion to a certain extent, and consequently is adopted to a certain degree in Nichiren's religion. Nichirenism emancipates religion from the dark interior of the church right into joyful human life. Therefore, for Nichirenians, religion is not only a religion in the ordinary sense but it is the principle and method of the synthetic creation of the world. And also for such reasons they establish religion as an achievement, the Heavenly Task.

Thus those who recognize and believe the Heavenly Task, in other words, the establishment of the Holy Altar in future as the vital point and signification of their lives, are ruled by those ideas, viz. absolute adoration, gratitude, mutual admiration of the same minds, vow to realize the law, and sacrifice of one's life for the law. These five are indeed their radical rules, which they willingly obey. And therefore they guard and extend the Law with all their powers, that is economical power, science, preaching, labour and so forth. They do not discriminate men according to

their ranks or occupations or races. Every man is
equal before the Heavenly Task, so they admire,
respect and thank each other for the practice of the
task. Therein lies their real worthiness. They believe
they are realizing an ideal human life in the society of
one another, if ever.

2. MODERN NICHIRENISM

As I have mentioned already, nearly seven hundred
years have now elapsed since Nichiren's death. The
development of Nichirenism, however, was unfortunately checked by political oppressions. During
these long years, therefore, his followers were forced to
keep silence *vis-à-vis* the public, thus causing gradual
stagnation. Because if a man is the true Nichirenian
he will denounce the people and the government who
are in favour of heretical religions. Consequently if
the government adopts a despotic administration,
then, as a natural conclusion, the government is sure
to interfere with Nichirenism. Indeed there have been
continuous oppressions and persecutions of Nichirenism
which led to the submersion of its followers for these
seven hundred years long.

But since the Meiji era Nichirenism has risen before
the public with its awakening and tolerance by the
Constitution. Nichiren's religion was thus revised for
the first time after his death.

However, the rise of Modern Nichirenism is due to
Tanaka's advocation. Nearly half a century ago,
among the multitude of the laity, a revolutionist, in
the person of a young man of eighteen years appeared.
Chigaku Tanaka was the man. He tried to revive pure

Nichirenism owing to his being self-taught in Nichiren's Works, and he at last denounced erroneous conceptions of doctrine and religious practice and also tried to abolish superstitions which arose during the troubled seven hundred years. The appellation of *"Nichirenism"* was coined and adopted by Tanaka for the convenience of recognition of Nichiren's thought and faith apart from the traditional conception of the appellation of *" Nichiren sect."*

At first he was overwhelmed with persecutions and abuses by monks and people, so at that time he was called a *Second Nichiren*. But his constant efforts have brought enlightenment to them step by step. He is still in good health and continuing researches, writing, lectures and other tasks. A few years ago he established a joint-stock company for the object of the spiritualization of industry according to Nichiren's idea of the synthetic creation. Lately he has engaged in dramatic works in order to make his views popular. He writes plays and at the same time he acts a part in his own person with his family and disciples. He organized the " Kokuchūkai " (The National Pillar Society) in order to strengthen the union of his followers. He also takes part in political movements according to the principles of Nichirenism.

Under his leadership many prominent scholars, for instance, Nagataki, Yamakawa, Hosaka, Shimura and others are devoting themselves to researches, propagation, writing, education, etc. His society is composed of a typical league of the laity only. On the other hand, many priests, monks and believers in the sphere of the old denomination were aroused from their torpor day by day ever since Tanaka's warning was proclaimed.   Honda, Shimizu and others are also leaders among them, and all of them are endeavouring to realize Nichiren's ideal at the risk of their lives.

Thus, modern Nichirenism is now rising. Its future extension doubtless depends upon the efforts of Nichirenians and their comprehension of the essence of Nichirenism as well as of the problems of the world.

The following are some of the reference books published in recent times in Japan :

Dictionary of Nichiren's Works, Vol. III, written and compiled by Yamakawa, Nagataki, and many assistants, under the superintendence of Tanaka.

Nichiren's Works : Shishio-Bunko edition, Vol. I.

    ,,   ,,   Ryogonkaku edition, Vol. I.

Systematized Doctrine of Nichirenism, Vol. VI, by Tanaka.

Doctrine of St. Nichiren, Vol. I, by Tanaka.

Study of the Japanese National Principles, Vol. I, by Tanaka.

Nichiren's Life, Vol. I, by Anesaki.

    ,,   Vol. I, by Yamakawa.

    ,,   Vol. I, by Hotarusawa.

    ,,   Vol. I, by Funaguchi.

New Study of Nichirenism, Vol. I, by Satomi.

Nichiren's Religion and its Practice, Vol. I, by Satomi.

The Future Religion, Nichirenism, Vol. I, by Satomi.

Nichiren as a Man, Vol. I, by Satomi.

Philosophical Study of the Hokekyo, Vol. I, by Satomi.

Comparative Study : Nichiren and Christ, Vol. I, by Yamakawa.

Commentary on the Rissho Ankoku Ron, Vol. I, by
Nagataki.
Lectures on the Hokekyo, Vol. II, by Honda.

Psychological Study of Nichiren's character, Vol. I, by
Takashima.

It is proposed to translate the Hokekyo into German from
Kumaraju's translation, with a technical introduction and
notes by Satomi and Hunziker of Switzerland, as soon as may
be possible.

There are many other books of reference, as well as maga-
zines and a daily newspaper, "The Tengyo-Minpo" (Adver-
tiser of the Heavenly Task), which was started by Tanaka.

GLOSSARIAL INDEX

Sin, conception of, 76

" Six Ors," 86

Stupa, heavenly shrine, 37, etc.

State-ethnical = relating to a country and its people, 15

Suchness = the One Truth ; the truth of the universe, 35, 36, 69, 79, etc.

Sugata, one of laudatory titles of every Buddha, 39

Summum bonum = the chief or highest good

Sungoddess, The Ancestor of Japan, 83, 188, etc.

Supreme Being, 77, etc.

Sutra = scripture, or documents

Synthetic creation, composite, combined creation as connected and forming a whole, 5, etc.

Synthetically = taken together, in combination

Taho, a Buddha, 39, etc.

Tanaka, 12, 228–230

Tathagata, one of the ten titles of Buddha

Taxonomical = classificatory, 32

Teachings (Jap. Kyo), 51

Teleologism = doctrine of final causes, 32, 85

Ten Commandments in Hinayana Buddhism, 95

Ten Mysterious Laws of the Honmon, 90

Ten Worlds (*See also* Mutual Participation). i. Hells (Nārakas) ; ii. the Preta (Hungry devil) ; iii. the Animal ; iv. the Asura (furious spirit) ; v. the Human ; vi. the Heavens ; vii. the Srāvaka (content with learning alone) ; viii. the Pratyaka-buddha (self-satisfied, for oneself alone) ; ix. the Bodohisattova ; x. Buddhahood, 17, etc.

Tendai, one of the great masters, 15, 16, 19, 20, 32, 52, 65, 68, 72, 75, 81, 114, etc.

Tendai-Shingon Secret Sect, 117

Tenfold Commandments, in Mahayana Buddhism, 95

Tenfold Prohibitive Commandments of the *Bonmokyo*, 96

Tenfold Suchness, 36, 79

Theanthropic = both divine and human ; the divine in man, 85

Theocratic = subject to the government of God, 85

Theriolatry = worship of animals

Thirty-Two Signs, in Buddhist doctrine, 8

Thousandfold Suchness, 36

Three Ages, 50, 56

Three Benefits, 23

Three Great Secret Laws (Sandai Hiho), 66, etc.

Three mental viruses, i.e. anger, greediness, foolishness, 134

Three Principles. *See* Japanese National Principles

Three radical mysterious laws, 90, etc.

Three Thousandfold worlds, 36

Tokiyori, lay priest of the Saimōji temple ; one of the Shikken, who became a lay-priest in his later years, as was the fashion, and lived in the temple named Saimōji, 130, 137

Trees and Grasses, Buddhahood of, 159

Two Hundred and Fifty Commandments, in Hinayana Buddhism, 95

Validate = to make valid, or of force

Vasuvandhu, one of the great masters, 51, etc.

Vehicle. *See* Hinayana ; Mahayana